THE
HISTORY OF
ADVERTISING

40
MAJOR BOOKS
IN FACSIMILE

D0929269

Edited by
HENRY ASSAEL
C. SAMUEL CRAIG
New York University

A
GARLAND
SERIES

ADVERTISING

THE SOCIAL
AND ECONOMIC PROBLEM

GEORGE FRENCH

GARLAND PUBLISHING, INC.
NEW YORK & LONDON
1985

For a complete list of the titles in this series
see the final pages of this volume.

This facsimile has been made from a copy
in the Library of Congress

Library of Congress Cataloging in Publication Data

French, George
   Advertising, the social and economic problem.
   (The History of advertising)
   Reprint. Originally published: New York : Ronald Press,
1915.
   1. Advertising.   2. Advertising—Social aspects.
I. Title.   II. Series.
HF5823.F897   1985   659.1'042   84-46045
ISBN 0-8240-6739-8 (alk. paper)

Design by Donna Montalbano

The volumes in this series are printed on
acid-free, 250-year-life paper.

Printed in the United States of America

Advertising

The Social and Economic Problem

Advertising

The Social and Economic Problem

By George French

New York

The Ronald Press Company

1915

The William G. Hewitt Press
Brooklyn, New York

Dedicated to
Pilgrim Publicity Association
of New England

Apologia

In the modern revolution of business, advertising is destined to play a much greater part than its present suggests, even as the significance of the business revolution is not perceived, or being partially perceived, is underrated.

The application of advertising to business is as yet tentative. Its possibilities are not realized. Yet it is now of vastly more consequence than we can understand or estimate. It is changing all the processes of business, and most of the manifestations of social and religious life.

This book seeks to suggest what advertising is doing and what it will do. It is a cursory view. No other is possible. Among the sciences advertising is a maverick; it has not been corralled nor branded. Among the arts it is a stray lamb; not considered of consequence. Among the professions it is without place or rating—an intruder without credentials. In business it is a saint or a sinner according as it has distributed its largess.

As advertising has no established standards as a science, an art, a profession, or a business, it has no binding traditions and but few precedents to consider. It is pertinent, therefore, for every observer to follow his individual bent, to have opinions and express them. None can contradict, none can prohibit. The writer of this book has set down some of his ideas, and some of the ideas of others, in the endeavor to picture advertising as it is. He is quite willing to assume responsibility for all that seems

Apologia

beside the mark, and to credit the bull's-eyes to whoever may lay claim to them.

The study and observation of advertising is one of the more stimulating of the mental exercises this century challenges us with. It leads far into the future, though we do not have to go far into the past to lose its trail. It suggests great things—great changes in business methods, advances in the application of religion and the humanities to life, the general sharpening of the keen edge of living. Through it the greater sciences, the more subtle arts, the more splendid faiths, and the profounder sentiments, make a deeper impress upon our lives. By its means business is becoming a predictable science. It is a guest at every fireside. It is present at every wedding, birth, and death. It is the Frankenstein of our lives, and their good angel. We are not more free from it than from the atmosphere. It intrudes everywhere, and is everywhere a welcome guest. It is good and bad. It helps and hinders. It may be an economy or an expense. It is as fluid as life, but as fixed and inexorable as fate. It is as transparent as crystal, and as opaque as iron. It is what it is. I am trying to picture what it is—and what it does.

August, 1914.

[8]

Contents

1

Introduction

Advertising is a real part of modern life; there is almost no phase of living that it has not invaded. It is a great factor in progress. It has been a great influence for bad, but in some of its functions it is coming to be a beneficent force. When skilfully applied, it has a power over people which is possessed by no other element of business or social life, and it may be so used as to be one of the great agents of civilization.

That advertising has generally been used for business purposes merely signifies that its development has not reached a stage at which many people feel warranted in employing it to promote social, moral, or religious, ends. So far as it has been employed for the advancement of religion or morals it has been used in a business manner and for business ends—for the augmentation of audiences, the raising of special funds, the moving of selected groups of people for special and temporary purposes. Its principles have not yet been applied to the task of swaying people's lives in a fundamental fashion for permanent purposes.

Advertising has already exercised a profound influence upon the economic lives of a very large proportion of the people of all civilized countries, more notably those of America. The real grip of advertising upon the lives of the common people was mani-

[11]

Advertising

fested earlier and more strongly in America than
elsewhere. In England the popular response to advertising has more notably manifested itself within the
past two decades, while in France and Germany it has
not yet obtained that hold upon the imagination nor
become so vital a factor in the daily lives of the
masses as in the United States. In the other Latin,
and Latin-American, countries its work has scarcely
begun.

While certain lines of advertising have flourished
in England for many years, it is only within the past
ten years that what we may call retail advertising
on a large scale, has been the important factor in
trade that it was in this country for many years
previously. The invasion of Great Britain some ten
years ago by a group of American subscription
booksellers, and their spectacular success in selling
to the British people through advertising, was an
event of classic significance—a wonderful perform-
ance—and its history is in the nature of incontro-
vertible evidence as to the efficiency of advertising
methods in enterprises that involve the swaying of
great bodies of people. The details of this series of
transactions in advertising have not as yet been
authoritatively furnished by the men who were back
of the revolution in selling that swept over those
islands.

Three American book canvassers went to London,
with the fruits of their work in this country in the
form of certificates of deposit in the London banks,
looked over the field, formulated their plans, and,

Introduction

as their first definite move, went to interview Mr.
Walter, then chief owner and absolute master of the
great British Thunderer—the London *Times*—pro-
posing to him a coöperative campaign of bookselling
on a grand scale. Mr. Walter peremptorily declined
to consider the matter, feeling that it was not consonant with the dignity of *The Times* to engage in a
scheme of the character proposed. But the Americans
were accustomed to deal eventually with men who at
first absolutely declined to deal with them, and by
patient diplomacy they finally got Mr. Walter to
suggest terms that would induce him to take up the
proposition. He, in his turn, thought the Americans
had unwittingly opened the way for his escape from
their importunities. He resolved to put an end to the
ordeal to which he was being subjected—the extraordinary experience of having to listen to argument
intended to persuade the all-powerful manager of the
mighty *Times* to reverse his dictum. He said he would
consider the plan—would in fact engage in the business—if the Americans would, as a retainer and evidence of financial ability and good faith, give him a
certified check for £60,000. He did not imagine that
this was exactly the opening the Americans wished,
and was astounded when one of them asked to be
excused for a short time, and presently returned with
a certified check, which was handed to Mr. Walter.
That perfect flower of the modern Englishman
showed that he was a good sport, and promptly
signed the contract, though it is certain that he
would much rather have thrown the check into the

Advertising

fire if by so doing he could have escaped from going
before the British people with a scheme so novel, so
American, and, as he believed, so likely to fail. But
he reckoned without true knowledge of his country-
men, as well as without a just conception of the pli-
ability and wisdom of the plans the Americans had
formulated for their campaign. The following few
years saw a revolution in advertising and selling such
as had never been concentrated into so short a time.
The Americans took due account of the English tem-
perament, prejudices, foibles, history, social and
business customs, and appealed along agreeable, cus-
tomary, and racial, lines.

This series of bookselling campaigns drew the attention of the English as never before to advertising
as a great business force, but the lesson did not reach
the roots of retailing habits and methods. It remained
for another American to invade London with a great
department store, which he promoted by methods developed by the successful department store managers
in America. This happened some five or six years
ago, and, though the English have not even yet accepted advertising as an inevitable factor in successful merchandising to the extent, or with the abandon,
we in America have accepted it, they are among the
"most favored nations" in that respect, and will in
due time come to the plane of those Americans who
frankly base their hopes for profit and continuation
in business upon scientific advertising.

In France and Germany there is much advertising,
and in Germany especially there is high-grade adver-

Introduction

tising. In those countries, however, advertising is not yet considered a necessary fundamental in all lines of business, and has therefore a more strictly commercial significance than in America. In some of its elements advertising has reached a high state of development in Germany, where it is given great prominence as a branch of the graphic arts. But this feeling for art does not extend beyond the physical appearance of the advertisement, which is made in accord with the canons of art chiefly because it is thought to be an object of art, rather than, as in America, because it is recognized that observance of the elementary principles of art gives it a greater psychological influence over the reader. The insistence of the Germans for their art canons in all the manifestations of advertising has had a salutary effect upon advertising in America, and for that reason we are persuaded to count the Germans as among the progressive peoples in the proper development of advertising.

In no other country has advertising put its mark upon the people with anything like the intensity it has in America. Here we are slaves of conditions imposed by advertising. The economy of our homes has been revolutionized. So radically emphatic and inclusive has been this change that it is a matter of grave speculation as to what may be the ultimate social, moral, religious, and economic, effects upon the people.

When we take a little time to reflect, in the light of a generation ago, we cannot fail to be profoundly impressed with the sweeping radicalism of the change that has come over our lives with respect to the economy of living. If we take an inventory of things we are compelled to purchase for the maintenance of life, with all its necessities and luxuries, we shall realize how completely we are enthralled by the advertised articles. It is quite impossible to buy many of the things in the form to which we were accustomed in childhood. Instead of going to the baker's and getting a bag of fresh-baked crackers, direct from the oven, hot to the touch, and delicious on the palate, we must be content with a carton of "biscuits," half the weight of our early-day bag, and less than half the quality, at two or three times the price. In this and in many other cases advertising has forced us thus to increase the cost, and diminish the quality, of living. Whatever may be said for the sanitary sealed package (and there is a good argument) there is no escape from the conclusion that we are paying more for many of the necessities of life, and getting them in a form devised by advertisers without our consent. Whether or not, on the whole, we are receiving greater value with these things that advertising has imposed upon us is one of the problems concerning which there is a mass of expressed opinion, but little conclusive evidence.

Whatever may be the record and responsibility of advertising in the matter of the increased cost of living, its effect upon life and happiness has been of a graver nature in other directions. It has been responsible for the introduction into living of a great

Introduction

many elements that are confessedly damaging. Take
the whole range of "patent medicines," so-called "proprietary articles," a large proportion of patented
devices and processes, the "cut-priced" sales of the
big stores, and innumerable things that are useless as
adjuncts to real life—they are to be included in
whatever indictment we may be inclined to draw
against advertising. There is so much output from
the ignorant and the "suckers" that it seems allow-
able that there should be some kind of a scramble for
it. The blame is fundamentally with the people who
go about with their purses open to the view of ambitious and thrifty collectors. Our consolation is that
advertising, as a profession, is taking effective cogni-
zance of these conditions, and that as a consequence
they will disappear in the not distant future. But
they have prevailed long enough to have materially
affected our lives, and they have bred up habits that
will continue to influence the lives of our children and
children's children; to puzzle and confound the sociologists and psychologists, to deflect and modify
our posterity; and to discredit advertising in the
minds of observers who do not go to the root of the
matter.

It is difficult to form an adequate conception of the
harm that has been done through advertising in fostering the purchase of things that are not only of
no real benefit to people but are a positive damage;
such, for example, as the many "sets" of books that
have been sold on the instalment plan through profuse advertising, mostly in magazines and weeklies.

Advertising

These books are not in themselves especially harmful. They are usually sold at too high prices, and under pretenses that are essentially false. From the point of view of good literature, good history, correct science, or useful and timely general information, they fall below what should be regarded as a reasonable standard of excellence. Some of the sets that have had the largest sales, and have made great profits for their exploiters, are old and out of date. They may have been subjected to "revision" which scarcely sufficed to remove the taint of age and inefficiency. They are cheaply made, and sold at prices that are too high for value given. Through the help of liberal, and not too frank, advertising they have been sold in great quantities, and the homes and minds of the people loaded with "literature" unworthy the name and not up to the claims made for it.

The matter of patent medicines has been pretty well discussed and ventilated. Their advertisements are barred from some of the better magazines and newspapers, but are still admitted to many periodicals that have large circulations among people living remote from the centers of population; and their promoters make use of advertising methods of their own. This particular evil, practically created and continued through advertising, is likely to disappear. The fact that reputable publications are barring patent medicine advertising is helping to kill its use. The more potent cause that is operating to discredit it in the minds of the people is the recent great reform in medicine, so far as the simplification of its

[18]

Introduction

methods and the growing knowledge of the people is concerned.

Side partner of this matter of the cure of distempers and disease goes the matter of diet, and here also advertising has much to answer for—more now than ever before. It cannot be said that in the matter of foods we are making great progress, or that advertising is, as a whole, very much less culpable now than ever. How large a proportion of the food preparations that are sold through advertising are fit to be eaten is a question that even Dr. Wiley, or Alfred McCann, might not be able categorically to answer. The methods of the poor food seller are subtle, skilful, scientific, and inexorable. Recent scientific discoveries have made an entirely new line of frauds possible. Our foods are now corrupted in such skilful fashion that it is quite out of the power of buyers to protect themselves. It is impossible to know whether an article of package food is prepared as it should be or as it should not be, except by chemical analysis. The new brand of syrup, or sugar, or breakfast food; the ham, bacon, sausage, beef, pork, poultry, fish; the flour, meal, bread, cake or pies; the spices, salt, flavorings, jellies; the canned fruits, vegetables, and other fundamentals of our foods, may be, and often are, so "doctored," in substance or manipulation, as to make their sale and advertising partake of fraud, in greater or less degree; and all of the element of fraud, whatever it may be, is fostered and imposed upon the buyers through advertising—that is, to the extent that the material and the state-

[19]

Advertising

ments about it are insincere, deceptive and fraudulent.

In many ways that cannot be specified, because this study is not intended as an arraignment of advertising but as a justification of it, advertising has contributed, and is contributing, to moral, physical, and economic degradation. To assume less would be to adopt the methods of deceptive advertisers, and to neglect a phase of advertising which, while deplorable, does exist.

In any fair view of advertising it is to be claimed that on the whole it is becoming a beneficent force in life, and the very distinct tendency is toward such use of its tremendous power as shall contribute to the betterment of life. This view is shared by a large and rapidly increasing portion of the advertising profession, and a larger number of professional advertising men are yearly coming upon the platform declaring that the only good advertising is that which works for the good of the people who are to read and be influenced by it. Many of the grounds for criticism that have been referred to are already passing beyond debatable consideration. Most good advertising men condemn patent-medicine and all other advertising that is not constructive and moral in its nature and object, and use their influence against it. Most good periodicals take the same ground, though many of them still make reservations in favor of the advertisers who pay good rates and give large contracts. Not all publishers can bring themselves to quite ignore that vile old legal maxim, "Caveat Emptor."

Introduction

The most promising factor in advertising at the present moment is a disposition to regard it as a positive and militant power for good in the world. The passive morality that bars fraudulent and deceptive advertising is already regarded as not the best attitude. Beside barring bad advertising there is a disposition to encourage advertisers of staple goods to inject a welfare element into their announcements —show that their goods may be used for some benefit to the buyer other than the economic and utilitarian benefits; how they may, for example, be made to contribute to the happiness of the family or the solidarity and sociability of the neighborhood, even though such use may apparently not only not increase sales but possibly limit them.

When all is said that can be said for advertising as a moral or economic force in society, it is to be remembered that all of its recent devotion to ethics and economics does not suggest anything more, or higher, than that it is seeking to relieve itself of a certain odium that has accumulated against it as the conscious assistant to unworthy efforts to dupe or defraud the people. The new devotion to truth and the fair deal does not contemplate much other than a return to the lines of the most obvious, the most perfunctory, honesty. "Thou shalt not steal" applies to advertising, and advertisers are just getting in a mood to acknowledge their obligation under the commandment. "Thou shalt not bear false witness" has been as vital for a time long prior to the existence of modern advertising as now, though advertisers are

[21]

but now slowly coming to a realization that false and misleading advertising comes under the ban of this law. When all advertising is brought up to the standards of the idealists, it will be merely honest.

II

General Principles and Methods

History does not inform us of a time when there was not advertising—the effort of some people to induce some other people to buy something or do something. The desire to influence the actions of their fellows seems to have been the motive that gave rise to the origin of written language. The first known symbol is thought to have originally signified a desire for coöperative effort. This motive has shaped the world. If men did not coöperate there would be no men.

Advertising is invitation to coöperate. The advertiser invites his readers to take some specified action that he believes will result in benefits to himself. To make his appeal plausible and effective, the advertiser usually alleges his ability and willingness to benefit the respondent—the moved reader of his announcement. Thus is set up the principle of coöperation. It is this power or disposition to benefit the readers that constitutes the attraction power of the advertisement. And it is the measure of fulfilment, on the part of the advertiser, of the implicit and implied promises of the advertisement that fixes his moral status.

This principle has become so operative that it is regarded as uneconomic to publish advertisements that do not rest upon the ability and willingness of the advertiser to keep faith with the people who read and may respond to his appeals. Thus it happens that the value of the square deal in business is being demonstrated through that branch of business that has, in its formative period, done as much as any other to corrupt the whole field of business, and instil in the minds of that portion of the people who are exclusively purchasers a feeling that it is the chief office of advertising to mislead and deceive and defraud.

While the principles upon which advertising rests have been ingrained in the constitution and practice of the people since prehistoric times, it is only since the middle of the nineteenth century that there has been anything approaching a separation of those principles for the purposes of modern advertising. The art of persuading people is a product of these times, and it is yet in a very crude state of development.

What is meant by advertising is something very different from the definition of the latest dictionary —"To give public notice of; to announce publicly, especially by a printed notice." This was the idea of advertising in the old days, when the merchant was content to print the fact of the arrival at his store of a shipment of New Orleans molasses, or of Scotch ginghams. Such a conception of advertising is now not only inadequate, but false and misleading. It is now one of the minor functions of advertising to announce or give notice. Its major function is to persuade.

Principles and Methods

Merchants are now sellers in a radically different sense from that of a less strenuous time. They used to offer goods, and await the necessity or pleasure of the people. They supplied the necessities of the people, but the people themselves developed their needs and nursed their propensities to purchase. They visited their merchants when there had been developed in their lives certain necessities. They bought goods because they had been made aware of the emptiness of their larders or the wearing out of their clothing. The new things they bought were needed to supply the places of those consumed.

The motive of advertising has changed. It is now the reverse of that which the dictionary notes, and that which animated advertising in the older days. Its office now is to develop the need or the desire. It ignores the necessity, for the most part. At the best, the necessities of the people form but one of the less considered elements of advertising, as it is now understood and practiced. The advertiser bends his energies to the task of persuading people to purchase his goods. He does not inquire whether there is a real need for his goods, and usually he does not concern himself about their utility in economic life. He often not only manufactures the goods, but, through his advertising, he essays to manufacture the demand for them—to create, in other words, a necessity in the lives of the people that has no economic or moral basis in fact.

Not all advertisers are animated by a motive like this. Some of them attempt to seek out real needs and cater to satisfy them. But whether the motive is to seek out real needs or to create fictitious needs, the

What he and his successors did for you

Milk is the most necessary single article of food in the world, but milk is more susceptible to contamination than almost any other food. It is essential that milk should be plentiful and accessible, but it is equally essential that it should be pure.

The man who first realized these facts and then invented the processes which made it possible for the entire world to have pure milk at any time, in any quantity and under all conditions, was Gail Borden. He invented condensed milk, he introduced the system which takes care of the milk from the cow to your cup in its pristine purity, a system preceding strict governmental regulations but found in accord with them when introduced.

Gail Borden left behind him an organization that has grown to be the largest in the world for the handling of milk, an organization inspired by his zeal, his honesty and his ability, an organization which has made his name a synonym for milk—fresh—condensed—evaporated —cultured—malted—every form of milk, but always pure and always good.

Borden's Fluid Milk is delivered fresh on the two largest milk routes in the world, one centering in New York, and one in Chicago

MILK

Borden's Eagle Brand Condensed Milk has successfully fed and raised more infants than any one single prepared infant's food in the world

BORDEN'S CONDENSED MILK COMPANY
NEW YORK, U. S. A.

Almost a Model Advertisement

motive for modern advertising runs along the attempt to persuade people to consider and buy the goods advertised, rather than merely to give information regarding the receipt or nature of goods advertised.

The present estimation of advertising is that it is a means for getting people to a sense of the proposals of the advertisers—a method of influencing people to subordinate their own judgment to the suggestions of the advertisers. The great purpose of almost all the present day advertising is to persuade people to do that which the advertiser wishes them to do, rather than serious attempts to picture to the minds of the readers the nature and advantages of the things advertised.

It is but a few years since this fundamental of advertising was discovered and put into practice. At first it took the form of what has been known as the "command" in advertising, and its first manifestation was the coupon. When the late Ralph Tilton, a son of the famous Theodore Tilton, devised the coupon to use in connection with advertising he marked the turning of advertising from the informative to the persuading phase of its development. When it was found that people would obey the command of the advertiser, expressed in the wording of the coupon, and would cut off, fill in and forward, the little forms, the advertising profession was given its first lesson in that rapid and marvellous development which has brought it distinctly within that rather new science of psychology, as it has recently been developed.

The coupon seems like a very crude and obvious device. It is usually couched in imperative language.

Advertising

It consists of a direct command to the reader to fill in his name and address and mail the coupon to the advertiser *at once*. The time command is very imperative. Nothing is left for the judgment of the reader. He is impressed with the idea that if he delays or dallies he will lose something in the nature of a special providence.

The coupon at once proved its remarkable efficiency. It brought returns such as the most sanguine advertisers had theretofore not dreamed of. It became all the rage in advertising. So effective did it prove, and to such an extent was it used, that it became the subject of official attention on the part of the postoffice authorities, who were inclined to take a hand in the regulation of advertising for the purpose of preventing the United States mail becoming a party to fraudulent advertising. The size of the coupon, compared with the size of the advertisement of which it formed a part, was restricted to not over one-fourth of the total area of the advertisement.

The almost automatic response to the coupon set shrewd and progressive advertisers to thinking. They sought to discover the secret of its power. Why should people respond to the stark commands of the coupons when they did not respond to illuminative descriptive advertising of the same goods? What was there in the circumstance that could be utilized in other phases of advertising and selling? It was at this juncture that the theories of some of the more thorough students of advertising—that it is closely related to psychology, and that the principles of

Principles and Methods

Forms of Coupons Used in Advertising

psychology indicate to the advertiser the way he must go to win popular favor—began to attract attention.

Previous to this time there had been a few men who dimly perceived that in psychology there is to be discovered the key to advertising. These were advertising men, not professors of psychology. The professors were slow to respond to what was manifestly a great call. They were inclined to sniff at the suggestion as being in the line of an application of science to business, and therefore, if not positively unethical, at least undignified. Let the business men discover their own panaceas, they said, in effect. The advertising men who had got an inkling of the worth of psychology to their business were looked upon as cranks, and dreamers of crazy dreams. But they persisted, and when the coupon revealed its marvellous and almost uncanny power, they saw the way to make their theories practical.

Yet it was some years before the professors could be interested, and some years before many of the advertisers who were coining money through the use of the coupon would admit that it was anything other than real magic that brought them the big returns. The men who taught psychology were ridiculed, and they did not know how to justify their faith. Psychology was yet to them the science of the soul. They had not perceived that it is really the science of the mind, and that its sphere and methods are as definite and easily comprehended as the sphere and methods of physics or biology.

Principles and Methods

In examining the nature of psychology, and its impact upon business problems and methods, some inspired grubber hit upon the hypothesis that psychology and physiology are intimately related, and advanced to the suggestion that the physiological theory of the motor principle of the mind, the office of the sensory and the motor nerves, the constitution and functioning of the brain, might be made to explain and account for a new and more reasonable theory of the effect of advertising upon people. This led to a recognition of a fundamental principle of the mind—its structural habit of assent.

Here was a reasonable theory to explain, not only the coupon but advertising in its larger application. It had escaped the notice of the advertising experts that it is inherent in the human mind to consent; that it is not natural for it to negative any proposition that comes to it, but that a negative impulse must proceed from deliberation and argument, and be brought about through distinct effort.

Nine-tenths of life is assenting, without thought, reflection, or argument. The other tenth comes after reflection, and after argument with our own minds. When we feel compelled to say *no* to any proposition, we find that we have first to debate the matter with ourselves, and bring ourselves to the point of saying *no* to our minds. It is not so with the larger proportion of our thoughts and acts. We assent to the major part of the mental activities required of our minds as automatically as our muscles work when we are walking. We are not conscious of any resolve to set the left foot in front of the right foot, or vice versa. Neither are we conscious of any mental effort of decision preceding nearly all of the assenting processes of our minds. We are, however, distinctly conscious of efforts to formulate a negative decision.

The theory of the motor principle of the mind is not only the most interesting psychological fact that advertisers have to consider, but it is the most important. A thorough understanding of it indicates exactly the nature of the problem the advertiser has in mind, and shows him the way to its solution, or to the conclusion that he ought not to waste time seeking a solution.

All this has found its way into advertising practice so recently that it is not yet well understood, and enters so imperfectly into the work of many advertisers that its influence upon the bulk of advertising is not evident enough to satisfy reasonable demands for proof that it actually is the fundamental it is assumed to be.

There are many advertisers whose comprehension of the principles of psychology is so hazy that it has little effect upon their work. There is a disposition to adopt the principles in part and in part to reject them. Some advertisers strive to minister to the sense of beauty, and make their advertisements good to look upon, but neglect to provide the convincing copy to follow up the introducing quality of beauty. And there are those who rely upon good copy and take little pains to have it slip into pleased consciousnesses over the oiled way of physical beauty.

Principles and Methods

The circumstance that this inclination to seek a relation between advertising and this subtle science of the mind has but just begun to manifest itself in operative advertising lends to the present condition of the profession much of its interest, and suggests reasons for considering it as something in addition to one of the more important factors in modern business. In that relation it is of sufficient importance to attract to itself much attention. With the passage of each year it is more and more evident that publicity is the foundation of selling. In contradistinction to the old attitude of inquiry on the part of the buyer, the present-day purchaser makes of himself a rela tively inert factor. "Where can I find what I need?" was the anxious inquiry of our grandfathers and grandmothers, whereas we are all from Missouri: We require to be shown, and we are not willing to move out of our tracks, or make the least effort to open our minds. Salesmanship must force our attention, and force us to exercise our option of choice. This it does through advertising in the modern manner.

It is this modern manner of advertising, the most recent conception of advertising, that brings it into the field of sociology in a very important way. Since it has been demonstrated that advertising derives its force and influence through its relation to psychology, and is able to induce great numbers of minds to take such action as it dictates, it is manifest that in advertising there resides power that may be as successfully applied to other activities of life beside business; that, in fact, we soon find it necessary to

appeal to advertising—adopt advertising methods—
for the promotion of every progressive and purify-
ing factor in life.

The significance of such a view (and it is imminent
in the mind of about every progressive person who
has given it thought) is tremendous, and tremendously interesting. It foreshadows a revolution in
ethics and religion, in education and erudition, in art
and science—in life—that is little short of terrify-
ing, so radical is the change that we recognize as
inevitable. If this extraordinary conception of the
force and capacity of advertising, and of those functions of science that have come to light through
advertising, is able to withstand the assaults of continued application in business it is inevitable that it
will be applied in other manifestations of life.

It is of interest to note the beginnings of the application of advertising principles and methods to religion, for example, and to note also that along with
the application of advertising methods to a series of
revival meetings—to cite something specific—there
goes also some of the peculiar moral atmosphere that
has always enveloped advertising and to which moral-
ists have strenuously objected.

In a certain city there were revival meetings going
on. The attendance was limited. The audiences were
small. There was not much public interest. People
could not be induced to attend. Somebody advised the
manager to make use of an advertising device. It was
announced that tickets of admission would be issued,
and that after a certain hour no more tickets could

be had and the doors of the hall would be closed. The announcement did not state that there had been more people wishing to enter the hall than it would hold, but that was the inference. The psychological trick was successful, and the hall of the meetings was for the remainder of the period filled without further effort.

Did the end justify the means? Was it honest advertising? Some means to fill the hall had to be adopted or the meetings must have been abandoned; the very same situation as confronts a great many advertisers. They must get the attention of the people, and they must arouse in them the buying impulse, or they must close their factories and abandon their enterprise.

Not long ago a certain religious society needed a certain sum of money. It tried all of the usual methods, but failed to get the money. A publisher of a paper offered to guarantee the amount if he were given money enough to do a certain amount of advertising in his paper. A man drew his check for the cash, and the publisher turned in the whole amount needed, after having expended for the advertising only three-fifths of the sum of his guarantee.

It is not too much to claim that a majority of successful movements involving the coöperation of people, undertaken for religion, ethics, or sociology, are promoted to successful consummation through the methods of advertising, applied consciously or unconsciously. But, as in the case of advertising itself, most of these applications are half-hearted compromises. They are tentative and timid, where they should be comprehensive and courageous.

It is fair to assume that it is advertising that has led the way into this new application of science to the influencing of people to follow a leader or adopt an idea or act in prescribed ways. It is fair to credit the selling spirit with having blazed the way toward the adoption of a policy of promotion for all good objects that is bound to work a great and significant revolution.

While we see clearly that all lines of social, religious, and ethical endeavor are benefiting by the adoption of the newer ideas of promotion, the fact that we do not so clearly see is that in consequence of this brotherhood in promotion there is coming into being a brotherhood relation between business and ethics, or religion, which is to signify much more to the world.

Much to the surprise of both, business and religion find themselves about to work hand in hand. From discovering that the material progress of business and religion may be equally promoted through the use of the same methods and by the application of the same principles, we have come to suspect that these deeper manifestations of life have an affinity that brings them into similar relations in our lives, if they are not indeed fundamentally the same.

It seems probable that we shall soon come to regard these two major manifestations of our lives—business, and the group of emotional elements we subdivide as religion, ethics, and morals—as having such intimate relations that we will ultimately cease to consider them as different elements and to apply to them different standards. And, again, it is necessary to credit advertising with having led us to this conclusion — that business is religion and religion is business.

In the course of their investigations and experiments the advertising men who have seen visions have discovered that one of the surest roads into the minds of the people to whom they wish to sell goods is along the lines of exact and uncompromising good faith. The discovery has been made that truth is a great business asset. It is not known how this came about, but since some three or four years ago there has been a great gathering of the clans of advertising around the standard of truth, and the clamor in advocacy of it leads to the suspicion that the advertising men had not previously been aware of the fact that truth has the power to make men free.

While the naïve welcome accorded to truth by the advertising men may provoke the cynic's smile, the fact is sufficiently indicative to cause us to look about for reasons and to prognosticate results.

What is to happen when business finally accepts the proposition that it is more profitable to tell the exact truth than it has ever been to throw a false halo about the goods offered? When the Golden Rule becomes a maxim of business as well as the shibboleth of the Sunday school, where will we be at? The comforting reflection is that this consummation is at hand. While we may acknowledge that there is a vast amount of fustian in the assumption of sanctity on the part of the advertisers, it is true that there is already a separation of those who really mean to live by the protestations of the newer morality and those who seem to use it as a cloak for their old habits of deception. The business itself is dividing the sheep from the goats, and, what is more to the purpose, is branding the goats so that they may not find it possible to pass as sheep.

Advertising has led the way into a new life for all business, and a new alliance between business and the gentler and more consequential phases of life. It is, of course, to be acknowledged that advertising has not created these conditions, and also that the enactment of this rôle has not been a matter of prevision on its part.

The most that can be claimed for advertising is that it was chosen as the medium for the introduction of this new era. It was fitted for the work, because it was compelled to seek for a way into the minds of the people, and when it found that way—when it was seen that people could be swayed and influenced through appeal to their automatic minds—the road to the utilization of this knowledge for higher purposes than the sale of merchandise was obviously open; and the lifting of the motives and processes of advertising was as inevitably obvious.

Advertising has promoted this new power over people to the full extent of its promised benefit to business, and no further. Advertising has advanced toward a brotherhood with religion and morals just

Principles and Methods

so far as it seems profitable for it to go, having always in view the ultimate and permanent benefit to business conditions and methods.

Every business exists for its own promotion. It is not open to anyone to criticise advertising because it is not more interested in the promotion of churches than dry-goods stores. It is for the church people to sit at the feet of the advertisers and learn how to make the churches bloom and fruit, even as the automobile factories at Detroit. And the churches are beginning to do it. They are emerging from the halo of their great purpose and taking thought of their usefulness in terms of promotion. They are learning of advertising how to get into the minds of the people they wish to move, and how to apply their principles so that they will take root and bear fruit.

But the significance of the new appreciation of promotion principles by business, and by those activities that have not the business motive, is not so much that there is here and there concrete evidence of the drawing together upon the same platform, as that there is such satisfying evidence that the two parts of a man are being understood to be in reality one.

That the churches have begun to think about their usefulness in terms of business, and that business has begun to think about itself in terms of ethical justice, is what gives warrant for anticipating a regeneration in social life the consequences of which we are able only to imagine. That a man who wishes to be as good as he should be, and do as much good as he may, can indulge a hope that the day is not far distant when he can be the same man in his church and in his counting room, is a consummation of the new spirit and the new knowledge in advertising that entitles every advertising man who has seen the light to consider that he is of a company of the elect.

How much less important it is that large sales of merchandise are made than that people begin to see life sanely! If the merchant can see that full weight, 100 per cent quality, fair prices, good service, and brotherhood, are the practices that are likely to bring him more and better business, it surely is well. If the churches can be made to realize that they can make life better for more people if they adopt the methods the advertisers have discovered and formulated for them, that is something to rejoice about.

Advertising, we see, if this view of its activities and genesis is correct, is something in the nature of a medium in which the varied elements that are at work to pull the world up to a higher plane are brought to a union, like a chemical union, producing the amalgam of that civilization we dream about and hope for. It neutralizes the natural acidity of man in business, and it stimulates the man in religion. It is a glass through which all men see things alike. It is a melting pot of present-day motives which will blend those motives—similar, though conflicting—into a composition that shall ring out a new note in the progress of mankind.

In fairness it must be said that advertising men are not conscious of the ultimate goal of their work. They see that it pays them better to accept the new

estimation of their business, and to point their efforts
toward the moral qualities that are becoming so attractive to them. They are quite willing to believe
that they are highly ethical, and to regard their business as founded upon the naked truth, so long as that
policy makes their advertising more effective; or so
long as the advocacy of such a policy contributes to
their bank accounts as well as to their reputation
among men.

Your real advertising man is an opportunist of
very high potency. He is early divested of his ideals
and enthusiasms, and fixes his eyes firmly upon the
penny that owes no allegiance and that may be lured.
He is learning the lesson that it pays to be truthful
and honest, and truth and honesty are his catch-
words. He loves them, and he loves to see them blazoned upon the sky, at so much per electric bulb. Here
and there we find an advertising man who is really
devoted to his shibboleths; and we usually find him
poor, and struggling for a foothold. Now and again
we meet one who is both able and wholly honest, as
well as firmly adhering to the new doctrine. If he is
able enough he has business, and is in the way of
becoming noted and notable. There are a few operative advertising men who have given themselves to the
new doctrines with whole-hearted zeal, and have become the apostles and prophets of the new régime.

The new advertising is passing through that
crucial period during which any propaganda is in
danger of being ruined by its professional advocates.
Nothing is so popular as moral shibboleths. The big

word "Truth" is bandied about as though all men
had been its advocates from the beginning of time,
and as though it means a succulent mental morsel
that has only to be swallowed to insure the regeneration of the whole being.

The principles of advertising have become expo-
nents of something that is to work a revolution in
business and morals, and be the means of building up
religion in the hearts of men. The practice of advertising is as sorely in need of these new principles as
is any department of business or any attitude of life.
It is permeated with a subtle dishonesty that is difficult to characterize and more difficult to eradicate.
There is in too large a proportion of current advertising a percentage of untruth that does not
harmonize with the exalted office the profession is
performing for the benefit of the best ends of civilization—untruths of reservation as well as of statement; all contributing to the building in the minds of
the readers of impressions that are not in accord with
the facts.

But the newer views will sometime eradicate even
this subtle quality of deception, because it is as dan-
gerous to the real welfare of the advertiser as is more
flagrant falsehood. The new lesson demands that the
advertisement shall create in the mind a true picture
of the thing offered, and of the conditions of the
offer, not that there shall be in the advertisement no
flagrant falsehood or misleading assertion. The advertisement, to be effective as well as moral, must put
a perfectly accurate and true idea of the thing ad-

vertised into the mind of the reader. Nothing less will square with the pretensions of the advertising profession, or with the new conception of the possibilities and responsibilities of advertising. Nothing less will, in the long run, be effective and bring the maximum of definite and continued results.

III

Science and Art in Advertising

Is advertising a science, an art, or merely a branch of business?

This question has agitated some of the advertising men, and has been discussed in the advertising periodicals. Though interesting, it cannot yet be answered with authority.

It is easy to deny that advertising is either an art or a science, as it is easy to assert that drawings or paintings of certain "artists" are not art. There are many advertising campaigns that show such skilful application of several of the sciences, particularly of psychology, as to cause the fair-minded critic to hesitate before he declares that they are not as fairly entitled to be called scientific as is the work of the chemist, the astronomer, the physicist, the surgeon, the biologist, or the physiologist. And the physical features of many advertising campaigns are so happily and artistically worked out as to create doubt whether any other practitioner of graphic art should be more rightfully entitled to the term artist than is the man who creates the finest of the advertisements. Both work from the same fundamental point of view, even considering the commercial motive. The painter hopes to sell his work, and the maker of the advertisement expects to be paid. The painter works according to certain canons, principles, and rules,

[44]

established as fundamentals. The maker of the good advertisement adheres to the same fundamentals, and works out his conception in the same hope—that it will appeal to the sense of beauty that resides in the consciousness of the person who sees and examines his product.

Like all manifestations of science, advertising makes use of those principles and rules that are common to all sciences. It recognizes them, studies them, and applies them in its products. It is the same with chemistry, with medicine, with biology.

The mere fact that advertising has a motive which directly demands money, in the form of business, instead of money in the form of fees, salaries, and less direct business influences, is a distinction that has led many to classify it as merely a branch of business. But would these same critics so classify the work of Edison, for example? That great inventor is without question a scientist—one of the greatest in the world. Yet he works for a direct business result; always for the purpose of making money from the specific thing he has in hand. The writer who would deny that Edison is a great scientist would discredit his authority and veracity.

The first definition of the word "science" in the Century Dictionary is: "Knowledge; comprehension or understanding of facts or principles." The second definition is: "Knowledge gained by systematic observation, experiment and reasoning; knowledge coördinated, arranged, and systematized; also the prosecution of truth as thus shown, both in the ab-

stract and as a historical development." The third
definition is: "Knowledge regarding any special
group of objects, coördinated, arranged, and systematized; what is known concerning a subject, sys-
tematically arranged; a branch of knowledge: as the
science of botany, of astronomy, of etymology, of
metaphysics; mental science; physical science; in a
narrow sense, one of the physical sciences, as distinguished from mathematics, metaphysics, etc." The
fourth definition is: "Art derived from precepts or
based on principles; skill resulting from training;
special, exceptional, or preëminent skill." The fifth
definition is: "Trade; occupation."

These are all of the definitions given to the word
"science" by the Century Dictionary. The Standard
Dictionary and Webster's International both give
substantially the same definitions, though both in
their analyses of the word give some definitions more
favorable to the advertisers. Richardson, an old English lexicographer, who published his dictionary in
1858, and whose aim was to trace the origin of
words, says that science is, in its origin, similar to
skill, and goes on to say that "science is knowledge;
art, power or skill in the use of it."

While it may be a fact that but little of the advertising that appears in the public prints ought to be
classed as scientific, it may also be claimed that much
of the writing about other sciences is open to serious
doubt as to its authority and truthfulness. No advertising man who cares for his profession enough to
assume that it is a science will claim that there is

more than a small proportion of its manifestations that are worthy of consideration as being scientific. Yet he will not admit that this fact disqualifies him from claiming that his product is scientific.

That in the best advertising which brings it within the purview of science is its very clever and original application of some of the principles of psychology, and its careful regard for the optical teachings of physiology and psychology. Not many of those advertisers who make the most skilful use of the teachings of psychology in their work are willing to acknowledge their indebtedness to the science that has had to endure the scoffs and jeers of unthinking people.

Ten years ago nothing would arouse more hilarity among any group of advertisers than to suggest that either of them was thinking about applying the principles of psychology in his practice. The unlucky wight who had been delving among the vague and abstruse books upon that science then extant became the butt of the crowd, and whatever sound argument he might be able to offer was laughed at. Then men did not know why they laughed, and the embryonic psychologist did not know why they should not laugh.

As in other lines of industry, the scientific elements in advertising have been translated into the vernacular, we may say, for the benefit of the workers in the business, and to relieve them of the peculiar distaste all workers have for naked science. The president of an art school, for example, delivers a series of lectures upon "Principles of Advertising Arrangement," instead of upon "Art and Psychology in Advertising." This latter title would have correctly described his lectures, while the one he used was not quite germane to his real purpose. It was justified by this feeling of aversion to frankly accepting science and art as possible concomitants of modern business and occupations. Another course of lectures by another college professor was called "The Principles of Appeal and Response," a not very accurate synonym for "Psychology," since the lectures dealt with psychology as applied to the arrangement of the physical elements of advertising. These elements of the psychology of the advertisement are among the principles of that science themselves subordinate in nature and application. They are not fundamental as original elements, but are sub-elements of the chief initial element of psychology.

Nevertheless, there has recently grown up in the practice of the better advertising men, especially with those who deal with the problems of large advertisers, and the better agents, a mass of expert knowledge about the effect of advertising upon people, under differing circumstances of salesmanship and differing degrees of necessity among people who are advertised to, which has become very valuable as a guide. Much of this information is undigested. It rests in the minds of the men who have worked it out from their practice, and is, so far as the general business of advertising is concerned, dumb and inexistent. It has been harbored as a personal, or corporate, asset, and jealously guarded from the knowledge of others in

the business. Some of the men who have been regarded as geniuses in the way of copy-writing, for
example, could easily reveal their secrets to other
bright men, if they chose to do so. Their facility,
which may rest upon the purely mechanical working
out of the principles of psychology, is assumed to be
individual, the expression of a talent comparable to
the ability to write verse or construct jokes. With the
great growth of the associational idea, within the past
five years or so, some of this guarded talent is being
opened to general participation, and the consequent
added respect for psychology as an advertising asset.

Art, as a controlling element in advertising, is also
coming into its own. It has had a like experience with
psychology. It is not now accepted in its naked
power. It is obliquely acknowledged. Yet its power is
so obvious that it is coming to be taken at its own
valuation.

Is advertising an art? It is, and it is not. It is an
art so far as the preparation of the advertisements
is concerned. It is difficult to imagine an advertisement worthy of being printed that shall not conform
to such canons of art as satisfy the discriminating
demands of the eye. It is here that the real efficiency
of the advertisement begins. If it has not the quality
of attractiveness it will be passed over by the eye,
and will therefore be of small account. The primary
fact about the advertisement is that it must attract
attention. In an ordinary Sunday newspaper there
are some 2,500 separate advertisements. Most of
them are not interesting enough to induce the ordi-

Advertising

nary man to look at them. And he must look at an
advertisement if it is to be productive.

The application of the principles of art to advertising is nothing more than common sense. There is
nothing of the mere love for art in it. It is simply
that the advertisement may be noted, by the people
who are idly turning the sheets of the newspaper or
the pages of the magazine. The wise advertiser never
considers art except in this way. Therefore the wise
advertiser is anxious to know what elements of art
will aid him in his desire to attract attention. He
knows that his advertisement must have the qualities
of a picture, and of a picture that is at once attractive to the eye. How is he to construct this picture,
within which there is his message to the reader?

Clearly, he must construct his advertisement in
much the same manner, and according to much the
same canons and rules, as the artist uses in the early
stages of his work, in painting, etching, water-color,
pen- or wash-drawing. There is nothing simpler, or
more obvious; yet there are many astute advertisers
who still make merry over "art in advertising."
When pressed, these Doubting Thomases are fain to
confess that they believe the writing and display of
advertising is just a matter of knowing people—just
a matter of human nature, you know. Precisely, it is
just a matter of knowing people, replies the advertising student. That and nothing else. Then he adds
that all the rules and principles of art are nothing
more than the formulation of accumulated knowledge
of human nature—attempts to formulate that which

THE CONSTITUTION OF THE UNITED STATES OF AMERICA

★ ★
★

BOSTON AND NEW YORK

HOUGHTON MIFFLIN CO.

MDCCCCXI

Proportion, Balance, Symmetry, Tone

Advertising

is necessary in any kind of composition intended to attract the attention of the people, and please them.

When therefore the accomplished advertising man talks about form, proportion, balance, harmony, symmetry, tone, color, etc., as elements of the good advertisement, we are to assume that he has in mind the construction of an advertisement that will attract attention, and that may avoid the fate of that forlorn 75 per cent of advertising which the statisticians tell us is abortive. From the standpoint of the reading public, all of the advertising printed in newspapers and other periodicals should be made to conform to such primary rules of art as will make it endurable to the eyes. Since practically all of our periodical literature owes its existence to advertising, and relies upon it for its profits, it is surely incumbent upon the publishers to make the advertising at least tolerable to the sight.

There is here a suggestion of one of the peculiar embarrassments in advertising. It is not possible for the advertisers to get the attention of the people they wish to address except through the operation of a selling element which predisposes many people against the advertisements, *per se.* The publishers of periodicals sell their subscribers a certain amount of literature, of some kind. They do not sell them advertising. They do not acquire from their subscribers any right to ask them to consider the advertising. They sell so many pages of reading matter, and they wrap in the package certain other pages of advertising that the readers do not contract for, and in many cases do not want. Yet the readers must receive the advertisements.

The advertiser is put in the position of the sewing-machine agents who have learned to coerce the house-wives to listen to them by means of putting their feet inside the doors and preventing the annoyed women from closing them until they have heard the selling story. The advertisements come into houses without the permission of the householders, and with no warrant other than the consent of the publishers.

This is an academic view, but there is in many homes a sentiment something like this unwelcome for the advertisements that are thrust upon them. It is seconded by the irritating sense that they are actually paying the publisher for his privilege of entering their homes to justify the sale of the wares of his advertisers, whereas he should be paying them.

The plea of the publisher that he could not afford to print and circulate his publication if he were forced to depend upon the money received from subscribers does little to mitigate his offense. He, not the readers, fixes the price of his publication. If he sees fit to offer it at less than cost, it is his privilege. It is his privilege to ask a price that will pay for the literary section of the periodical, and a sufficient profit; and then it may be his duty to strictly limit the advertisements he accepts to such as may reasonably be expected to benefit his readers.

It is one of the fictions of publishing that people will not pay a fair price for periodicals. They do pay for certain ones a price sufficient to cover the cost and provide a profit. There are a few publishers now trying the experiment, with newspapers and other periodicals, and it is not unlikely that in the not distant future it will be possible to read the news of the day, and purchase an adequate supply of periodical literature, quite free from advertising. Why should all advertising be located upon the public domain; along the highways, in the street-cars, in papers and periodicals bought for another and very different purpose than to read the advertisements? 'Tis a Utopian idea, and far from probable realization, though there are some indications that it may seriously be accepted. But if the advertisers and publishers wish to continue to enjoy the free usufruct of the highways, the street-cars and other travel opportunities, and the pages of the public prints, it is clear that they must study the public limit of tolerance, the tastes of the readers, and force advertising practice into methods that are not obviously distasteful to them—make the advertising more artistic; more tolerable, in its function of the unbidden guest.

There are many advertisements that are artistic in their make-up. There are many that are designed to attract as though they were artistic. It is one of the misfortunes of America, where the advertisement is so profusely universal, that artists have given little attention to it. In Germany the best artists take a hand in designing advertisements. In England men with good reputations as artists do not scruple to design advertisements. In America a few artists condescend to draw figures for advertisements, and a few

Science and Art

good designers can be prevailed upon to make lettered pieces for advertising purposes. But the figures that the good artists draw, and get big prices for, and the fine pieces of lettering made by good designers, are at the mercy of advertisement constructors, many of whom do not know how to relate the artistic units with the other elements in such a manner as to produce artistic objects.

There is hope in the situation. Progress has been marked during the past few years, and there is some movement toward a real understanding of what art and science can do for the advertisement, even if the ultimate verdict is against the dictionaries that advertising is not a science and not an art. It is not possible to deny that it is a trade, or a calling; nor is it possible to deny that it is one of the more interesting of callings, dealing as it does with the delicate and responsive attributes of human nature, and depending upon the response that can be wheedled from people by playing upon their innate love of form and color and eloquence, and their instinctive faith in whatever their fellows may tell them as truth.

It is possible that this need of knowledge about advertising, which is of late so insistent, may eventually lead advertising interests to attack this problem of classification in a constructive manner. Events are leading toward some organized attempt at research and organization. Nothing is more necessary than some orderly attempt to place advertising among the professions. Enthusiasts have been urging systematic research and assimilation for the purpose

Advertising

of ascertaining to what extent advertising may draw from the stores of the other sciences and arts. Until something of the sort is done, and the results made known, there will be none so rash as to claim that in its practices advertising is an art or a science.

There is little agreement in method and practice. There may be an advertiser in Philadelphia who makes a very careful study of psychology, tries to ascertain the facts about the people he wishes to reach, and endeavors to apply the principles of art to his advertisements. He gets good results. There may be another advertiser in Boston who employs nothing in the way of art principles or psychological findings, but just the "rule of thumb," and he also gets good results.

One man in Detroit who alleges that he has made a study of the whole matter, and who reinforces his statements with many tabulated results, lays down some rules that are radically at variance with the findings of the professors of psychology in the universities. One advertiser asserts that there must be expended for advertising not less than two per cent of the total receipts, and another shows that he has built a big and profitable business, entirely by advertising, with an expenditure of less than one per cent of his gross income. Yet another alleges, with perfect truth, that he has expended a fortune for advertising and is a bankrupt in consequence.

Such varying results would not be possible if scientific principles prevailed in advertising practice. There is nothing approaching science or art in much of the current advertising, and there is in the consciousnesses of most of the advertisers no sense of their need of art or science. There is, in other words, little attempt to know the people the advertisement must appeal to, and little attempt to make the advertisement appeal to anybody beyond the man who pays for its insertion.

Science and art in advertising show how a particular people may be interested, and how to so make advertisements as to insure their interest for a majority of people reading certain periodicals. There is in the advertising business no room for "art for art's sake." There is nowhere room for art for art's sake. Such art is inconceivable. There is art which gives pleasure, and has no other mission, and there is the love of art because it is good art. Art is nothing unless it appeals and instructs and ennobles. It is to arouse within us the finer and better emotions that we love art. If it did not so affect us we could not care for it. In advertising it is because we must arouse some emotion in the people who read that we wish our work to be artistic. If we hope to arouse favorable emotions we must know the people to whom we are appealing, and that is the office of science. We must know how to appeal to the sense of beauty through the eyes of these people, and that is the office of art.

If we dissect our thought about art, and define it to our minds as architecture, painting, etching, modeling, sculpture, drawing, engraving, etc., we find it difficult to conceive that advertising, or printing, or bookmaking, can be art. But if we go a step further with our analysis, and try to define to ourselves what it is in those forms of art that appeals to us and makes us delight in them, we may discover that they are formed of elements which must be dominant in advertising, printing and bookmaking, if those industries are to produce things that please us; and we find that when the advertisement is constructed according to the canons of art, as the painting is constructed, we feel the same sense of pleasure in the one as in the other. We may discover that that which especially attracts us in a piece of imaginative literature is some form of words that appeals directly to our individuality—agrees with our experience or expresses our sentiments; and we may discover that some advertisements attract us in exactly the same manner.

It is thus that the advertisement partakes of art and science in like manner as the water-color, the poem, the essay, or the story. Advertising that has these qualities is as rightfully entitled to be called scientific as the essay, and artistic as the painting. Neither is art, neither is science. Both are artistic and scientific. The work of the investigating chemist is scientific, and so also is the work of the advertising man who knows and respects, and makes use of, the same common principles of science and canons of art.

IV

Who Pays the Cost?

The ideal view of advertising is especially interesting, because it suggests a force that is capable of profoundly modifying life, and is modifying it to a degree that is not generally realized, invading its every phrase with a silent, steady persistency that seems, when considered in connection with its unvarying potential success, almost uncanny. It is also a wonderfully ductile and efficient agency for the promotion of business. We see great factories rise, and great fortunes built up, as the results of an inexorable policy of pushing upon the public goods that the public had previously no idea that it either needed or wanted.

A fertile-minded man conceives some novel form for a common food, for example, and begins to manufacture it. There may be no demand for it, and no necessity for it. Nobody knows anything about it. The same food is available in a different form, and possibly a better form, and is sold at a more economical price than the new product can be sold. The new food costs just as much in its raw state, and there has to be added the cost of the new process of preparation, the fancy package, the selling and advertising, and a profit large enough to yield the promoter a fortune in a relatively short time—if he succeeds in his advertising campaign.

The key to the situation is the advertising. If it is

so skilfully done as to lead people to buy the stuff, the problem of the originator's fortune is solved. The consumers get a fancy package of ordinary food, treated by grinding, steaming, or some other process, to appear different. It tastes different, and it is delivered in "sanitary sealed packages." All the germs and dirt that may have got into the ordinary product, that had been eaten from father to son longer than the memory of man runneth to the contrary, are barred, and some of the work of the digestive organs is avoided—possibly to their detriment.

This process, or some process resembling it, is applied to a wide range of the necessities of life, and advertising is made to float them. None but the people with economical and analytical minds realize the extent of the dominance of advertising in modern life, nor what it means as an element of the much discussed high cost of living. It is not alone the articles that are advertised but the policy of advertising that has made it possible to box and process certain products and get from 50 to 150 per cent more for them, that has induced that method to be adopted in the handling of many products that are never advertised. It used to be the custom to get smoked beef, for example, shaved from the big chunk as wanted and at a reasonable price. Now it is usually sold in packages, shaved by machinery from we do not know what kind of a piece of pickled and scantily-smoked beef, packed in packages of unknown weight and sold at the rate of two or three times its value. A small carton weighing three ounces is sold by grocers dealing with the poorer classes of people at 12 cents, which means 64 cents a pound.

There is a great variety of foods treated in this way, and some of them are priced tremendously above their value, above what they can still be purchased for in bulk. A favorite device is to get a product so well known as to be practically standardized and then reduce the bulk or weight of the contents of the carton while gradually adding to the price. There are standard products in the market which have thus been made more costly to the consumer within a few years to the extent of 15 per cent in price and 12 per cent in bulk, while the price of the raw material has in the meantime declined not less than 25 per cent. This means that the people who buy these products were gradually forced to pay at least 50 per cent more than a fair market price, and at least 25 per cent more than the same thing could be had for in bulk.

This disposition of the retail market, which runs all through the different lines of materials necessary for householders and housekeepers to constantly buy, and constitutes a very onerous tax upon them, is not to be directly charged to advertising. But advertising is, in a very real sense, responsible for the custom. The wonderful development of advertising has taught what can be done with people, through the methods suggested by psychology. If advertising has suggested to the makers and dealers this onerous policy, that sin will have to be charged against the greater possible benefit that has already flowed from the intimate contact with and control of the masses of people. There has never yet been devised a sure preventive for putting beneficent principles to the use of people who wish to deceive—stealing "the livery of the court of heaven to serve the devil in."

This particular evil will some time be cured by the same force that encouraged its parturition—advertising. Some fine and glorious day it will dawn upon even these men who are prostituting the principles of good publicity that it pays better to cater to the welfare of people than to shrewdly rob them under the pretense of benefits. When that time comes we shall find that there will be a return to those practices that inure to the economic benefit of the buyers, and our smoked beef will again be served at our groceries as of old—sliced from the honestly cured round of beef and sold to us at so much per 16-ounce pound, sans multiple wrappings and pasteboard cartons; and the package of sausage will have another link to compensate for the two ounces filched from the package we have a right to suppose is a pound, and the several unnecessary wrappings.

Advertising, through its recent development and the principles of psychology it has brought to the front, has shown men who sell how to sell for more money. That is the gravest charge that can now be made against it. Advertisers themselves have taken generous advantage of this discovered willingness of people to be led up to the financial sacrificial altar. They have been "piling it on" during the past few years.

The scientific men of the colleges are of the opinion

that advertising contributes to the high cost of living, and their contention is exceedingly difficult to combat. All that is left for the advocates of advertising is to justify it; and it is no small task to justify it, considering the array of facts that can so easily be marshalled—the crushing array of facts. As an economic proposition, it avails little to show that an advertised article is sold for less than it could be sold for if the advertising that had been done for it had been omitted, and the sales therefore had been very small in comparison.

It is generally felt that advertising is something of "a gamble," and that therefore the advertiser is justified in figuring for an excessive potential profit. So many advertised articles are special, patented, or in other ways held by the advertiser for himself, as against the trade in general, that he is in control of the selling price.

A percentage of advertising is in restraint of competition, by reason of exclusive ownership, or some device or method intended to give the advertiser a peculiar advantage over others handling the same or similar product. This exclusive element is often utilized for the purpose of getting excessive prices from the buyer. In advertising this is excused and condoned in various ways.

The advertiser of a new thing is not certain of getting a sale sufficient to justify a moderate profit. He figures that he must get his money back on the basis of a possible small sale. So he adds a large margin to his costs, and when he finds that he is selling liberally he keeps the big margin for the purpose of accumulating a fortune, as the reward of his acumen and industry. If a patent conflicting with his own patent is granted, he fights it, or buys it up for a quiet life in his safe; thus protecting his trade— and his patrons. Advertising is his warrant and his protection. Possibly he began to advertise on the credit of some publisher or advertising agent, but when the time comes when the public manifests a curiosity about his business methods, or a rival seeks to market a product at a lower price, he points to his advertising expenditure, intimating that he has sacrificed all these thousands, or hundreds of thousands, for the definite purpose of bringing the excellencies of his product to the attention of all the people.

The stark financial fact is that all of the advertising that is successful is paid for by the consumers; and that all of the unsuccessful advertising is done with the hope that the consumers will eventually pay for it.

The question of the justification of the cost of advertising, from the point of view of the consumer, does not rest with the question of who ultimately pays for advertising. It is manifestly a good investment for the consumers to pay for some of the advertising that is charged up to costs by the manufacturers and dealers; and as to much of the advertising they pay for, it is as manifestly purely an expense for them.

There has been a vast amount of sophistical explanation of this question, "Who pays for the advertising?" But nothing has been brought forward to show that the consumer does not pay for all of it that is successful; and more remotely, and through more devious channels, all of the unsuccessful advertising as well is paid for by the general mass of consumers, though not by the particular class of consumers that was appealed to by the unsuccessful advertisers.

The real question about the cost of advertising is, of course, whether or not the advertised proposition has within it sufficient promise of benefit to the consumer to warrant that the cost of bringing it to his attention may be made a charge upon him.

The question of the cost of advertising, put in this way, is capable of being discussed upon economic grounds. Many interesting questions are involved. There is first the question of free will. Whatever disposition of advertising costs may be made, it is evident that the consent of the consumer to be charged with them, under any circumstances, is never solicited. He is an involuntary party to the proposed draft upon his money. The advertiser is virtually exercising that legal communal right called "eminent domain" when he makes a schedule of prices for commodities to include the charges for advertising, without consulting the consumer.

That the consumer cannot be consulted must rather be considered as adding to the responsibility of the advertiser than in the nature of his justification. If it is urged in justification, it is quite fair to suggest that the advertiser is inclined to hide his arbitrary acts behind that other legal shibboleth, hateful in any connection it is used, "Caveat Emptor." It is all well enough to cry "Let the buyer beware," but to justify even that barbarous legal maxim it should be considered that the conditions of which the buyer must beware shall be at least measurably under his control, when he, having perceived that he must beware of economic traps and pitfalls, wishes to exercise his rights of self-protection. A man cannot profit by this maxim when the conditions of the transaction he is invited to contemplate are fixed before he comes into it. A man strapped to a railroad track cannot profit greatly by the sign "Look out for the engine" when he hears the express roaring down upon him.

Therefore, while it is freely acknowledged that it is impossible to get the consent of consumers to have advertising expense charged to them, and that to suggest it is a manifest absurdity, it is also evident that a charge for advertising cannot be put upon the selling price of an article without by that act increasing the price of the article to the person who buys it. It is not competent to argue that if the article had not been advertised at all its price would have been even more. Whatever the price might have been for the unadvertised article, as against the price for the same article advertised, there would have been in it no percentage for advertising.

The justification of advertising expense charged to the consumer is to be sought elsewhere than in the specious, and often spurious, plea that the article would have cost more had it not been advertised. This is the usual plea of large advertisers, and that they feel obliged to make use of it is evidence of the weakness of their case or of their reason. We must come down to a more fundamental economic principle. We must examine the laws of value. If the advertised article is economically worth the price charged the consumer for it, there is no further question regarding the items of expense incident to the justice of the price asked. It does not matter that the selling price has to be made up of a series of cost items, one of which is advertising, if it is shown to be reasonable in view of the necessity that induces the buyer to buy and the utility the article bought may prove to be to him.

The progress of the world has been made possible through gaining the coöperation of masses of people. Coöperation is impossible until the people have been informed of the objects to be sought. Coöperative benefit in new inventions and discoveries, and through improvements in living accessories and conditions, is what advertising has to offer in this way. There are all the time coming on the market devices that are positively helpful—without which our rate of progress or our comfort would be materially limited and checked. It is necessary that these things shall be known to the people they may benefit. Advertising is the practical method for making them known. Without it progress would be exceedingly slow.

The safety razor, to mention a specific example, would have been known to but a small proportion of its present users if any other method than advertising had been adopted to market it. Now it is evident

Advertising

that not only a great number of individuals have benefited by the advertising of safety razors, but that there is a large communal benefit that has accrued in consequence of that advertising. It is no sufficient disclaimer to suggest that the marketing of these razors was, in its early stages, uneconomic, and that the price charged for the devices was exorbitant. It is true that the idea was rather wild, and the chances of failure large. The idea was new, and not likely to be accepted until after a long and determined campaign of promotion had been executed. In the early days the sales of safety razors could not have been much in excess of enough to justify the expense. There was then a time of large profits, which was followed by competition and price reductions that possibly brought the business in general down to a plane of profit that was not only not excessive but not adequate. One decade sufficed to squeeze all of the exorbitant profit out of the business, and witness the beginnings of the inevitable series of failures due to over-production and over-advertising. The great company of self-shavers brought to light by the advertising campaigns paid for the idea with the price of their first outfits. Looked at as the one transaction, they paid too much —more than the circumstances of the initial act warranted. They paid $5 for an outfit that might economically have been sold for less. They could not at once consume that purchase, and therefore exhaust its usufruct. Within a year or less that exorbitant purchase became an economy to them. Their savings

Who Pays the Cost?

on their shaving bills had more than absorbed the first cost of the razors, and instead of continuing to figure on balance sheets as an expense the original cost had become the cause of constant and considerable savings.

There are many advertised things that will show this kind of economy, if considered in the same true manner; and it is in this way that the cost of advertising must be reckoned and distributed over the balance sheets of the people who read the advertisements and respond to their invitations to buy. If it is not possible to apply this method to the results of advertising it is thereby made evident that that particular advertising is not economical for buyers, and that it does add to the high cost of living in an unwarrantable manner. It is the price of profitable knowledge that the wise advertiser of the worthy article exacts from the people who buy it, and it is usually a fact that whatever they pay for this element of their purchase is the lowest factor of their total bill. It is lost sight of by the critics of advertising that a large part of all the advertising that is done is for the purpose of giving consumers some valuable information; letting them know how and where, and at what price, they can supply themselves with things that will make for their comfort and happiness.

V

Misleading Advertising

It is very difficult to disguise misleading advertising. The cloven hoof generally shows. It is the very ignorant and the very credulous who are victimized. The majority of the victims are intent upon securing some unfair or unreasonable advantage. Readers of advertising take very long chances. The great advertising frauds have been based upon such ridiculous claims that it is a wonder a single person able to read would give them a moment's thought. But they do, and because they do their infirmity of judgment must be considered. It is as reprehensible on the part of advertisers to take the money of fools as it is for the common pickpocket to take the money out of the cup of the blind beggar. So, reputable publishers and advertisers are inclined to take drastic measures to protect those who have not wit enough to protect themselves.

It has been stated that there is in much of the advertising that has a reputable appearance an element of deceit that it is difficult for the sophisticated to detect, but the great advertising frauds are easily distinguished, and as easily avoided. Nobody but a credulous and avaricious person would pay the slightest attention to the mining and land announcements that have been bonanzas to their promoters and sink-holes to the people who "invested." There ought not to be a person in the United States, able to read,

Misleading Advertising

who will be so much a fool as to pay the slightest
attention to the patent-medicine and "cure" advertisements; but there are many who do, and who pay
money to continue and nourish their delusion long
after they have had evidence enough to convince the
most sceptical in almost any other phase of life.

Stupidity and cupidity explain the constant vogue
of the mining, land, banking, etc., advertisements;
and the fact that many people believe they are cured
by the advertised nostrums explains their continued
vogue. Many people *are* cured by these so-called
remedies, that have no actual value whatever. Disease
is so much a fiction of the mind that anything that
can arouse faith cures a long list of ailments that
owe their existence to the sufferer's belief that they
are real. While the "regular" doctors continue to
perform cures through making their patients believe
they will recover, so long as the Christian Scientists
do actually cure a large proportion of the cases that
appeal to them, so long as Dr. Worcester and his
aids in Boston are constantly curing people suffering
with very real diseases, no one can deny to the
patent-medicine men a share in the general mind-cure
business. The evil of their practice is, of course, that
they do not discriminate, and are always ready to discover diseases that their poor dupes never had sus-
pected and that exist only as opportunity to defraud.

When a gullible person sends money to an unknown person for an advertised article, not vouched
for by the character and policy of the publication in
which the advertisement appears, he invites loss—

challenges the regular order of affairs to reverse
probabilities that he may get something for less than
he knows the genuine article is worth. When a person
allows the cheap and manifest bait of the advertisement to obscure what little sense he has, he should
consider that the lesson he gets when he is fleeced is
worth the price, and turn his loss into gain by after-
wards keeping away from that snare.

Advertising has now been a feature of the daily
life of all people long enough to have bred in them
some degree of sophistication with reference to
it. But people do not learn to care for their interests. They probably never will. More than half of all
the people need to be always under the care of guardians. And the advertising interests have got to act
as their guardians, so far as harm coming to them
from advertising is concerned.

When all is said about the misleading character of
some advertising that can be said we find that it is
but a small element in the whole business. A large
proportion of the complaints arise from the contribu-
tory negligence and foolishness of the buyers. Advertising appeals to sentiment, and it must employ some
lure to attract favorable attention. In a sense, it is
impossible to conceive of advertising that will not
deceive somebody.

Men and women are not so constituted that they
will respond to a plain statement. They will not avoid
sudden death and total ruin unless they are persuaded. They will not seek salvation unless the delights of the future are painted for them in vivid

colors. If there is any excuse for advertising there is the coördinate obligation to do it in such a manner as to make it effective. If it is desirable for people to buy a certain thing it is necessary to persuade them to do so.

It is this extremely delicate and hazy line between justifiable and necessary lure for the justifiable purpose and the bait for the unjustifiable purpose that divides proper from improper advertising. It is sometimes almost impossible to draw this line. It is always happening that the true nature of advertising is not at first apparent, even to the expert and practiced eye and judgment.

Much of the criticism of advertising is due to the fact that its critics are not willing to allow that it must exercise lure. Those estimable people are willing to listen to the hyperbole of their pastors, to the soft and comforting talk of their physicians; they read with glowing approval the stories in their favorite magazines, and absorb the color given the news reports in their newspapers; they listen with smiling approval to the iridescent talk at the dinner-table, and tolerantly smile at the wonderfully inflated tales of "grandpa" who "fit into the war"; the ladies discuss their dress and their neighbors with certain definite embroidered effects, and the men dispose of their rivals in business and golf without exercising restraining choice as to adjectives.

But there is not a disposition to give the advertiser that privilege of colorful language and vivifying incident. His efforts must conform to a different standard. That is impossible. There must be that same lure in the advertisement as we insist upon putting into other phases and manifestations of life. If it were not the privilege of the advertiser to persuade people, why would he advertise at all? It is the office of advertising to entice, and how can that be done without lure in the advertising? It is not competent to argue that advertising may better be dispensed with than that it be made the vehicle of disingenuous adjectival allurement. If that position were tenable there would be no advertising question.

It is possible to arrive at a better understanding of advertising if we frankly regard advertisements as human documents, expressions of the aspirations, needs, plans, and ambitions of the men who write them, or for whom they are written. Then we would be able to understand some of the apparent inconsistencies of the advertisements we see in newspapers and magazines, and we would be able to consider them with a little more charitable understanding.

If we think of the artificial devices resorted to by people in their intercourse with one another, for the purpose of producing certain effects, favorable or otherwise, we may excuse some of the artificialities of the advertisements. People are "all things to all men." They must be. A person with pronounced character is not the same person to two of his intimates, and the more intimate his friends are with him the more variety they perceive in him. The speech of people does not convey the same meaning to all. It is modified according to the nature of the listener. It is

Misleading Advertising

not understood alike. No two people will get the same impression from a lecture, nor will they understand the statements of the lecturer identically. A great preacher will not instil exactly the same theological principles in all of his auditors.

This colorable quality of speech and apprehension which we recognize in people extends also into and over their expressions through other forms than speech — through their written thought, and especially in their correspondence. A man's letters reveal quite a different personality from that suggested by his speech. For some reason, it is much easier to write from the bottom of the heart than to speak from that locality. One can, and habitually does, write himself into letters to friends in whose presence he is dumb, or confines his conversation to the weather. Many a man who has become noted since death owes his posthumous fame to the letters he has written, or to a journal he kept all his life in profound secret.

The advertisements that are effective are parts of the personality of people. They partake of all this graphic personality. They are human documents. They have that peculiar interest which attaches to literary work; though, indeed, some of them are far enough from literature. They are entitled to a judgment different from that we would pass upon a salesman who should mislead us as to the composition and quality of a piece of textile goods. We are inclined to look upon the advertisement in a different light, because we know very well that it is only an invitation for us to come and look at the cloth. We feel that when we actually see the cloth, when a skilled salesman shows it to us, he will acquaint us with its exact qualities; and we, when we take it into our hands, look at it, feel its texture, test its strength, and play its tints in the sunlight, will be able to judge its usefulness for our purposes. Here we are right against all the facilities for the final tests, and if the salesman persists in trying to have us accept a view that we feel is not altogether right, or that is not fully sustained by the goods as we see them, we resent such treatment, and probably leave the place without making a purchase, and with a distinct dislike for the salesman.

But if this same salesman had met us at our office or home, and had told us exactly the same tale about the goods that he did tell us when we were examining the goods, we would not have resented it. So we do not resent the statements and implications of advertisements that make some attempt to paint the lily. We know it is the invitation to the sale, not the sale. We court the invitation, but we will not tolerate deception at the final moment of the sale, when it is necessary for us to rely to some extent upon the statements and advice of the seller. There is a vital difference between the invitation to the sale and the sale, and if that difference could be explicitly stated it would correctly characterize the advertisement in contrast with the sale.

The "truth in advertising" that we hear so much about is, therefore, a shibboleth that is to be taken with some grains of understanding. The truth that

Misleading Advertising

can be made the basis for advertising is not the same as the truth that must pass current as man to man. It is such truth as the artist observes when he paints a picture and arranges the details to appeal to sentiment, rather than graphic verisimilitude. The photograph of a horse in motion is without doubt anatomically true, but it is false to all that our eyes tell us of the horse in action. We never saw such grotesque actions, and as a matter of actual fact they do not exist for us. Which view of the horse in action is the true one? It is not the anatomical photograph. If we could have a photograph of the horse in motion taken with an x-ray outfit we would have another illustration of one phase of truth, but it would be strange and untrue to us, considered in the light of our lifetime of observation of the horse.

In accepting truth for ourselves we are compelled to rely upon our experience and observation. If some savant tells us that what we see is not in accord with the revelations or deductions of science, his truth is not the truth that we are compelled to accept as our standard. That in our lives is true which impresses us as truth. That is truth which we feel leads us most surely toward our ideals. That advertisement which impels us to consider the purchase of a handsome piece of goods for a suit or a gown, is for us more true than another that might give us an analysis of the same goods, for the reason stated—that the advertisement is regarded as the invitation to look upon the goods, and not as a certificate of their composition.

Advertising

We are not to be lured to anything, except duty, unless by agreeable means. The beauty of form and the beauty of groups of words are what we look for in the invitation of the advertisement, and those qualities are what contribute to truthful advertisements.

But the statements of the advertisement must lead to truth, and be, so far as they are specific, entirely truthful. It will not do to claim that wool is sealskin. It will not do to claim that ours is the greatest store in the world, when it ranks third on the street.

There is a mistaken notion current among certain advertisers that the lie obvious is good advertising. It is the worst possible. The lie inferential is almost as bad. It deceives nobody to say "Value $10" on the ticket that marks the goods at $4.98. This "value" shibboleth is one of the more flimsy of the flimsy devices of the untruthful advertiser. Some of the reputable stores that use it have evolved a most curious justification. They say that goods so marked have the value alleged if by thus marking them they can be sold! The *bona fides* of this attitude may be thought to be questionable. Would these advertisers wish buyers to understand the meaning of "value" as they explain it in their attempt to justify advertising in which it is an important element? Suppose they were to insert in their advertisements their understanding of the word they make such profuse use of!

The value of truth to the advertiser is very like the value of the modification of literal truth in the advertisement. It is most valuable as a shibboleth. It

Misleading Advertising

is worth much to the merchant, even while reckoning a big per cent of profit, to be able to say that customers are always told the truth about goods. It is worth much to have customers feel that they have always been told the truth in certain stores. There is nothing so valuable for advertising purposes. Frankness and openness sell goods.

The real meaning of the recent vogue of "truth in advertising" is that advertisers have made up their minds to do less actual and obvious lying. There is a difference. The truth in an advertisement may be dressed in an attractive garb of words or illustration. The lie is always stark. There is some justification if some of the ultimate truth is withheld from an advertisement, because the advertisement is not usually the ultimate seller. The lie cannot be so garbed as to be admissible. The lie in advertising is the selling crime for which there is no excuse. The effect of the lie in advertising is not to build up trade, but to pull it down and limit it. The trade liar is always well known, and he has always to work for new customers. His lying is his undoing. The lie in advertising works much harm to the ignorant and the gullible, and they must be protected. If the lie in advertising affected only the shrewd and the able it might be left to do its purging work. We are all ashamed of the impulse to take pennies from children or from the blind.

VI

Ethics in Advertising

The person who gets "stung" because he is credulous beyond the point of reason is quite certain that advertising is immoral. There is a lurking sense in the minds of many people that advertising is not altogether ethical. The professional men are certain that it is not. The advertisers themselves do not have entire faith in it as a means of demonstrating highly moral motives. The magazine men do not esteem newspapers as wholly moral in their advertising practice, and the newspaper men return the compliment, with interest added.

There is, it must be admitted by the most zealous advocate of advertising, a definite suspicion of advertising, as a profession, in the minds of a great many people whose opinion is entitled to respect. It is beside the question merely to say that this suspicion is not well grounded, that it is due to practices that have been abandoned by progressive advertisers, that it is unworthy the intelligence of up-to-date people, etc. It is there, in the minds of many people. It is in the minds of thoughtful advertising men. It is one of the most serious stumbling blocks in the way of those people who think they see in advertising methods a way to hasten the regeneration of the world, to promote every good project that needs the coöperation of many people.

To say that advertising is used to promote immoral

purposes is not to touch the reason for the feeling of distrust that is felt with regard to it. To recall that the merchants who use it do so for the purpose of exaggerating the value of their goods in the minds of people is not to account for its reputation. To be conscious that advertising has led thousands of people to squander millions of money does not touch the root of the matter. The feeling against advertising lies deeper than any of these items of criticism indicate. It is regarded as a sinister force in the world, by some right-thinking people who have not taken pains to carefully analyze the sources of their prejudices.

It is probable that advertising has, from the time that it became a factor in selling, been employed to lead people to do things that were not beneficial to them—that were meant to defraud or degrade them that the unscrupulous advertisers might gain. It is used in that mean way now, and probably will be so used for many years to come.

The advertising profession, as represented by its best elements and by the local and national organizations, is making a determined effort to make advertising more worthy of the respect of everybody, and to eradicate this feeling of hostility from the public mind. The forces that are resisting the movement are the old ones—money and power. Advertising has bred up a variety of methods for getting money without fairly earning it, and those methods will be held tenaciously by the unscrupulous and greedy. The great advertising mediums are in a position to make degrading and fraudulent advertising impossible, and many of them are trying to do so. But there is as yet a sufficient proportion that are unwilling to risk the loss of the income derived from the frauds to give the frauds opportunity to ply their piratical trade. It is difficult to conceive of a newspaper that makes the public welfare its great boast allowing the schemes of the plunderers through advertising to use its columns. Nearly all the important magazines select their advertising with the welfare of their readers in mind. There are yet several with great circulations that allow a variety of manifest frauds to operate through their pages. Why they do so is quite apparent: They regard the public that buys their magazines and reads the advertising that they print as a bounteous treasury from which they are licensed to draw as much revenue as possible.

The newspapers are leading offenders in this corruption process. While a few of them have "cleaned up" their columns, and will not take an order for advertising a manifest fraud, nor for advertising in a misleading manner, too many take whatever is offered. Some make a faint attempt at selection; will not take the most virulent of the frauds, but do not scruple to give opportunity to a choice aggregation of money-getting schemes and deceptive medical and financial advertising.

To visualize this matter let us take a certain big New York newspaper—one that does as much for the public good, on its editorial page, as any newspaper in the land. Without making any search for the worst

Ethics in Advertising

copy, we will take that dated the day this chapter is written. Without examining the small advertisements —the "classified" sections—we discover 27 advertisements that are clearly objectionable—medical, investment, liquors, and cigarettes. These advertisements occupied 1,352 agate lines of space. Reckon them at 25 cents per line (they probably average more) and we have $338 income for one day. At this rate this paper would be drawing $123,370 a year from this traffic in the money, health, and morals of its readers.

Let us assume that the advertisers in this paper spend about 5 per cent of their gross income for advertising. Probably they spend more, but to get an idea of the magnitude of the business we may put them on the basis of 5 per cent. Suppose that there are twenty newspapers used. A little figuring shows that the amount taken from the public, through the favor of the twenty newspapers, would be in the vicinity of $50,000,000 a year.

Fifty millions is quite a sum of money for the newspapers to have on their consciences. The question is, Do these newspaper proprietors have consciences? There are two of the biggest New York papers that have a great volume of this corrupting business, and all of them trifle with it in some form. There are but a very few papers in the country that do not. Just now it is a good self-advertising policy to be able to proclaim that a newspaper has decided to refuse to publish advertising of this nature. One of the New York papers alluded to, which is now printing nearly five columns a day of this objectionable

Advertising

matter, made an announcement some time ago that it had decided to become virtuous, and it printed a self-advertisement on another page stating that it "stands for the right" and "safeguards the homes of its readers," "protects them from imposition," etc.

There is creeping into the advertising business a conception of its power that has already begun to modify its practice, and may in time bring about a radical change. It is that advertising is necessarily a matter of good faith. It rests upon the word of one man given to another man—the statement of the advertiser to the reader. It is strictly a matter of good faith, for the simple and obvious reason that goods offered through advertising cannot be seen and examined. There is nothing by which they may be judged but the word of the advertiser. It is in the nature of man to play fair, and when there is no way of verifying one's word it is natural for the man who wishes to retain self-respect to at least approximate truth. The advertiser is, by reason of the conditions of his acts, put upon honor. The advertising liar is much more despicable than the verbal prevaricator, because the person lied to has no recourse. The advertising liar is not a good sport. He hides behind circumstance. He dodges detection by hanging up the receiver. He cannot be cross-examined. His raw statement goes unchallenged, and his hope is that some few gullibles will believe him.

Shrewd advertisers are learning that the sneak in advertising is not the party that "pulls down" big returns. So the advertising liar is gradually getting

Ethics in Advertising

to be discredited, as a business getter; and advertising generally profits thereby. As the truth that advertising is a man-to-man proposition becomes better understood, man-to-man principles become more favored. While advertising is the most impersonal of all intercourse, where the personal element is grievously needed, it is a strange thing that the most acute of personal principles seem destined to dominate it. "As man to man" is a very strong plea for true and fair treatment. With most decent people it will secure for him who uses it the square deal he wishes. It is coming to that in advertising.

The really great constructive writer and creator of advertising never even thinks of trying in the least degree to mislead his readers by any of the many tricks of manipulation of language that were, not long ago, the stock in trade of the copy men. He seeks for the briefest phrase, the simplest word, the clearest construction, the truest meaning. His attraction must be other than the attempt to paint the lily. He knows that his composition must not wear a mask. He knows that he must not lurk in the shadows of verbose avoidance. He knows that he has got to stand squarely in front of his readers, look them in the eyes, and deliver the straightest tale he can possibly construct—if he wishes his advertising to pull somewhere near 100 per cent of possibility.

That this policy pays best in the long run, for the advertiser who is trying to sell worthy goods, there is no longer a doubt. That its practice is gradually spreading is evident. That it will finally prevail we

Advertising

know well. When that time comes there will be an end to dishonest, misleading, fraudulent, and undesirable advertising. The reform must come from the advertisers. The publications are not constituted to attempt it, and the public, through laws and enactments of legislative bodies, cannot do it any easier than it can prevent ball-playing or chestnutting on Sunday.

The public can help, by getting a truer notion of what advertising is, and why it is. When the people realize that advertising is a purely business proposition, callous to ethics and esthetics, as such, they will have put themselves in a position to do effective work for reform.

The object of advertising is to make money. When its methods are radically changed it will be along lines that promise more money than it now yields. When it becomes generally known that clean and moral advertising pays better than the other kind, all advertising will become moral and clean. When it is conclusively demonstrated that other forms of advertising pay better than billboards, billboards will disappear, and the esthetics of the highways will be that much improved. If records show that car cards are not efficient money-makers, they will go the way of all inefficient advertising, and the street-car people can decorate their cars with more artistic and consistent schemes.

Despite all in the history of advertising, and all of the degrading attributes it has developed and nourished in modern business, it is manifest that advertising is destined to be the active agent of the most

Ethics in Advertising

significant and far-reaching reform in business the world has ever seen. There are now plain indications of what this reform is to be, and some hints as to what is to be the method of its approach.

We are now just able to seriously consider the union of business and religion, business and ethics, upon the same plane of life. The hard-headed business man is willing to listen to those who see that life is life, whether it is business, religion, ethics, morals, art, science, or altruism—all are manifestations of the same life, and all must yield allegiance to the same laws, the same rewards, and the same punishments. And underlying all, there is, and the business man sees that there is, the same great operative law that must ultimately control all human beings and all human activities—the law laid down in the Golden Rule.

The idea that goodness in business involves sacrifice, that the man who operates his business upon the principles he preaches in Sunday school must expect therefore to be a loser, has been ingrained in the nature of men. It is not easy to force the imagination to accept the great truth of the Golden Rule, and apply it to business, expecting that it will help in the game of making money. Advertising is demonstrating that business and religion must be promoted in the same manner if success is expected with either. The drawing together of these two phases of life, which have been considered radically different—antagonistic—is one of the greatest and most significant evolutions of human nature any generation has been

privileged to witness. It is advertising that must be
thanked for a large proportion of the new order.

Credo

for Advertising Men

* * *

I believe in advertising.

I believe in clean advertising.

I believe in profitable advertising.

I believe that advertising has a double function: To benefit the advertiser and the people advertised to.

I believe that if advertising does not benefit the people advertised to it cannot benefit the advertiser.

I believe that advertising cannot benefit the people advertised to unless it is truthful and clean, and employed only to sell goods that are genuine and offered at fair prices.

I believe that advertising employed to sell goods that are not beneficial, or goods that are beneficial but offered at unfair prices or on inequitable conditions, is wrong in principle and will, in the long run, be unprofitable to the advertiser.

*Written by George French for the National
Vigilance Committee, A. A. C. of A., 1914.*

Ethics in Advertising

We hear much about "art for art's sake," the devotion of people to art for the pure pleasure of being thus devoted, without hope of personal pleasure in art. Our devotion to religion and ethics has been about of that nature. We have been religious, on Sundays. We did not believe we could be religious all the week. Business was business, and religion was something quite different. Religion, with the best of us, was a cloak, not donned to conceal wickedness, but worn in the form of a cloak so that it might the easier be thrown off on Monday, and the easier donned again the following Sunday. We have had an academic belief in religion, and we have hoped that proper devotion to it on Sundays would help us on in the world that follows this. When it came to business, that was a different matter.

Now that advertising has demonstrated that it is more effective, makes more business, when it is truthful and honest and fair to the man of the other side, we have begun to realize that all business may be more profitable if it is conducted with regard to the rights of the other party to the deal.

This is not a matter of the humanities. It is a matter of cold business. Better and more business can be done on the platform of the Golden Rule than on the platform of Caveat Emptor. Advertising is gradually showing that this is true. The shrewdest men in business are gradually becoming the most zealous adherents to this new doctrine. Business is gradually becoming safe for the man who is not the selling expert, but the uninformed buyer. Men in business are gradually realizing that one sale to one man is the most uneconomic method of doing business—that one sale does not make an enduring business. The one sale must be the promoter of other sales, and to secure this result the one sale must be beneficial to the buyer. The Golden Rule must be the basis of every sale.

This policy, this belief, is coming into business, and coming rapidly. It was advertising that brought it into business, as a business element. The advertisers have been obliged to consider the people who buy. They could not locate their mart along the thronged ways of travel and expect that a proportion of the passers-by would enter and trade. They had to go out and get the people; and they had to go bearing promises. Advertising is selling seeking buyers. The advertiser must make some human appeal or people will not stop to read. Advertisers deal with the man before they can deal with the customer. To deal with the man successfully they have to deal with him urbanely. They have to cater to the man.

Advertisers first sought to win people by making promises. They found that they must also keep the promises they made. One promise might possibly bring one purchase, but if the promise was not fulfilled the buyer became an enemy. Not only did he not return to buy again, but he induced others not to buy at all. Advertising seeks to induce habitual buying. The first purchase is very costly to the advertiser. It is the second, the third, the continued trade, that brings the profit. If an advertiser can sell 100 suits of clothes as the direct result of one advertisement, he divides the cost of the advertisement into 100 parts, and reckons that each suit cost one of those parts to sell. He extinguishes the cost of the advertisement at once. But if ten of the men who bought suits return to the store for other suits, at other times, there is the profit on them to add to the sum that should properly be credited to the advertisement; and as long as any of those 100 customers, attracted by the advertisement, continue to trade at that store there is profit coming to it from that advertisement.

The profit does not get credited to the advertisement, which is all right. But the consequential fact is that it was the true statements in the advertisement, and the fair dealing on the part of the merchant, that attracted the continuous trade of the ten men, and made for the store an endless chain of profits. So the merchant argues that he will continue to print truthful advertisements, and give customers a square deal, because he sees that that is the best and least expensive promotion he can possibly have. He soon becomes a stanch advocate of honesty and the square deal in business, and some fine day he will understand that this policy of his is the same as his minister has, for all the years of his church-going, been zealously preaching. He sees that business and religion are the same, so far as they affect him in his every-day life. He goes to church to listen to the expounding of the principles of right living, and he goes to his business the next morning firmly convinced that he can carry those principles into all his transactions during all the secular week. He is landed squarely upon the platform of honesty and truth, because he has discovered that those are vital elements in his business. He would never, it may be, have come to that conclusion if his advertisements had not converted him to it.

This process has been at work in advertising for a long time. There always have been advertisers who have been entirely honest, but they have been conscious that they were not quite business-like. They have felt that they were sacrificing something to sentiment—that their business would probably have been larger if they had followed the custom of employing the lie in their advertising. The new advocates of truth in advertising frankly assume that it is the more profitable policy, and it has thus been carried into the general practice of a great many concerns, and the people who buy are the beneficiaries. It is a habit to tell the truth in advertising and in selling—not a universal habit, but getting such a vogue that we know it must become universal.

And it is a beneficent law of our beings that we finally become converts to our own policies. The man who is truthful because he thinks it policy to be truthful benefits all with whom he comes in contact; and if we confer benefits we are certain to receive some reward. So we get to believe in the truth, and to love and practice it for its own sake, through having practiced it as a business policy. Thus are the advertisers who adhere to truth in their advertising drawn further and further into the practice of co-ordinate virtues, immersed deeper and deeper in the ethical life.

Those who have followed the development of the convention idea among the different lines of trade and industry have noted how those gatherings have advanced from the strictly business and social gatherings they were, to the great inspirational and sentimental meetings many of them now are—devoted to the propagation of the cardinal virtues as the most effective trade tenets. The advertisers have led this development, the annual conventions of their club of clubs being little different, in zeal and sentiment, from the old-fashioned Methodist camp-meetings. Most of the addresses have for several years been little other than exhortations for truth and honesty and the fair deal. Their week of meetings has for four or five years been a round of fervid promotion of morality in business. They have preëmpted the churches in the cities where they have met, and their shrewdest men have gone into the pulpits and preached the purest religion, as the basis for their business of advertising. An impressionable person cannot attend one of these conventions without getting the conviction that if the millennium is not at hand there is a business revolution impending that is not greatly different in character and consequence.

The practice of advertising has led to this investigation of its springs, and has revealed the essential agreement between it and morals—between the principles of successful business and successful religion.

Advertising

It has bridged the supposed chasm between business and religion, and shown us that there is a common base upon which our lives rest, and from which all of their activities spring. It is not easy to estimate what this is to mean in the world.

VII

Social Effects of Advertising

The effects that flow from the advertisements as they are printed may be observed and estimated by every man for himself, since in this primary sense there is no authoritative consensus of effects, and it is all practically a matter of feeling, limited personal experience, loose generalization, or pure prejudice.

As a factor in sociology advertising has never been estimated or tested. There is a well-defined feeling among the more thoughtful and progressive advertising men that it is destined to work wonders in the line of practical social efforts and development. This feeling is not based upon anything more direct than the successes of advertising in business, and a meager series of inconclusive and tentative experiments in the field of sociology, but there is good ground for the faith that animates the prophetic souls of optimistic men in the business. There is nothing inherently improbable in the suggestion that many of the multiple aspirations of sociology and religion may be effectively promoted through the application of tested advertising methods—if these methods can rightly be modified for the purpose.

Perhaps it is too much to hope that people needing regeneration will at once submit to the demands of the advertising methods. "Do it now" is a potent command to bring responses to the soap advertisement, especially when accompanied with an offer of a set of dining-room furniture or a can of pickles. The preachers have been dinning the "Do it now" command into the ears of unregenerate people from time immemorial; yet there are many people who have not yet done it. Nor is the disposition to respond to such an appeal for such a purpose as strong now as formerly. If people were to be directly appealed to for the purpose of bettering their moral or social condition it is a matter of doubt whether it would be worth while advertising.

For the purpose of perfecting the machinery of sociological and ethical efforts advertising may be more directly useful and effective. It has proved a good method for raising money, for bringing crowds to meetings, for getting masses of people into the habit of wishing for some specific confirmation, and thereby putting their sub-conscious minds at work to devise means for its accomplishment, and generally to instil in the minds of the public an idea, or an interpretation of an idea, the application of which would benefit great masses of people.

There are yet not enough results to make a general conclusion possible. There must be more, and more consequential, results; and it is fair to assume that such evidence will soon be available. There is no doubt, as a theoretical proposition, that advertising will soon become one of the more effective factors in the work of the people who are assuming the task of making other people better, more moral, more orderly, and more productive of good.

Not one of the big movements for these purposes

but would vastly benefit if more pains were taken to let all the people know what they are doing and what they wish to do. If Mrs. Russell Sage, for example, would appeal to the people, in an effective and systematic manner, to help in her campaign for the preservation of wild birds she would find that there would be so much help offered that her actual accomplishments would be doubled, or quadrupled, without extra effort or more money. There are a great many people who would be glad to help on the work of the Rockefeller Foundation, or the sociological activities of Mr. Carnegie, if they were to be told exactly what these enterprises aim to accomplish, and were invited to join.

The sociological impact of advertising upon communities is much greater in another line, less known and more difficult clearly to indicate.

The practice of advertising is breeding a new variety of man. Consider the training it gives those who are immersed in it. Take, for the purpose of making the subject as concrete and vivid as possible, the advertising solicitor who is put into a certain field for the purpose of getting all the advertising for a popular magazine there is in its business potentiality. Assume that he is a bright, broad-minded, conscientious man, intent upon making a better record for business for his magazine than any predecessor has made, or than any representative of another magazine has done. He has read books upon advertising, reads the literature about business promotion, has his ambitions. He believes in the people, likes them, and has a sincere desire to promote their welfare. How does he proceed to get the business his managers demand from his territory? Does he go out and haunt the offices of the advertisers, singing the praises of his magazine, and begging for orders? He takes an entirely different course.

This advertising missionary proceeded to make a careful survey of his field. He found out all about the advertising accounts that are in evidence, and as much as possible about concerns that had manifested leanings toward advertising. He conceived that the people he would have to deal with were human beings, and therefore subject to influences based upon that fact. He found out about the civic organizations in his district, and especially about the advertising clubs. He became familiar with the churches, the church clubs, and in the course of his first few months of work he tried to discover the church connections, or leanings, of the managers of advertising accounts. He made the acquaintance of the newspaper publishers, and as many of the reporters as possible. Being a man with talent, and talents, he began to insinuate himself into gatherings, and now and then he made practical suggestions. He joined civic clubs, and at their meetings he made short talks, with a punch to them. Before long he was in demand for talks at functions, and always made a good impression. He saw his name in the newspapers, accompanied when possible by the name of his magazine. In these ways this mythical man insinuated himself into the social and business activities, and his name became well known.

Social Effects

The public estimation of his magazine was modified, for the better. It became, in that section, a better advertising medium, and advertisers were, insensibly but surely, disposed to think more favorably of it. Mr. Representative was careful not to urge attention to his magazine.

In his contact with the men who actually handled the advertising accounts, Mr. Representative was as diplomatic and wise as in his work with groups and organizations. He went over his district at a time when there was no advertising to be given out. He got close to all the managers, and whenever possible he met the wives and children. He studied every man, and tried hard to do each some substantial favor. He talked about their work, and was often able to give them valuable hints. Being really a high-class man, and a thoroughly good fellow, he soon had the warm friendship of about every man in his territory who had anything to do with advertising. He did not press them for business. He rarely alluded to orders. He did not brag about his magazine. When the occasion was right he had the knack of giving some pregnant fact about it that went straight to the mark. He gradually extended his range to take in some of the concerns that did not advertise at all, but which he thought ought to. He did not bore them about the benefits of advertising. He studied the men and the business, and at some psychological moment he planted his advertising seed; and it was always good seed, which he put into good ground.

He watched his field with untiring care, and he

[99]

Advertising

knew the workings of all the advertisers in it; he knew the minds of the men who handled the advertising; he knew, far in advance, plans for new business; and when the time came that some concern announced that it would see the advertising solicitors for the purpose of making its lists for the coming season, our Mr. Representative smiled quietly to himself. When the procession of anxious solicitors for the other periodicals was racing to the extreme of the district to try for orders, he took down his telephone and caught the manager before any one had seen him.

"Hello, George," he would say, "I hear you are ready to give out the orders you told me about last month. I suppose I get something."

(Voice over the phone)

"Yes, that will be all right. Thank you. How's the wife and the kiddies?"

(Voice over the phone)

"Well, isn't that fine!"

(Voice over the phone)

"I'll see you some day next week. Thought I would not bother you to-day. Good-by."

This man's business grew and grew in that district. He beat the other magazines in his class—and the other men, who wore out twice as much shoe-leather and spent twice as much for railroad fares, wondered how it happened. But getting the business for his magazine was not all that Mr. Representative did in and for that district. He got a great many people to thinking about civic betterment. He made a special hobby of housing, and talked it on every occasion.

Social Effects

It was a harmless topic, and about everybody agreed with him, because there was little prospect that anything concrete would be done. All the politicians enjoyed talking about something that would require a lot of city or state money. Yet there were some results. Some real estate schemes were turned in the direction of better homes for the working classes, and a big apartment house was erected in the congested section of one of the cities.

He soon got some of the other advertising men interested in his propaganda, and within three years of his advent there was a well organized bureau of speakers willing to go anywhere to talk all kinds of civic betterment. One always talked good advertising. Sometimes they went in squads, and did all the talking at some meeting of a trade or civic organization. The seed was sown everywhere where there was prepared or receptive ground, and there were noticeable results. Here and there a town would not respond, but in most towns there was a decided increase in interest in civic affairs, and some improvement in the conditions of life. The newspapers got the habit of printing full reports of these meetings, often with editorial comment. One of the chambers of commerce made an industrial survey of its field and published the results in a handsome book. The whole region was energized, some towns much more than others, but there was scarcely a hamlet into which this man, or some of his coadjutors, had not invaded with his message of civic uplift. Clubs of advertising men, church men, and just interested citizens, were formed in many places, and some of them continued the study of communal conditions year after year, with results that cannot be estimated.

This advertising man never existed, in just the form he is here pictured, but the advertising men of a region did do as much, and more, as has been indicated, and their work has done much to raise the standards of civic life in those states. Those men were working for their business. They hoped to arouse, among other things, more interest in advertising. Yet they were entirely sincere in their public work. They saw in it opportunity to impress themselves, and their publications, upon the imagination of the people, and they worked hard to do that. Their underlying motive was more or less selfish, but what of that? They did as much good as though they were devoted to nothing but the uplift of the people; probably more.

What this particular group did in its restricted field was being done all over the country, and is being done. Advertising men everywhere are vitally interested in the life of the people, in the conditions under which the common people are obliged to live, and the chances that are accorded them for their advancement, their convenience, and their pleasure. Wherever there is an advertising club there is likely to be some sane and vigorous work being done for civic betterment. Probably half the energy of all advertising associations is expended in that way.

It would be very difficult to estimate the results of this work, in order that the profession of advertising

might receive the credit that is its due. It is quite true
that the time was ripe for agitation in civics, and
that there were others besides advertising men working for the same ends. But the advertising men have
everywhere been leaders, and in many places the only
leaders. They have come to the front with plans for
definite action, and made demonstrations that have
effectively aroused many communities; made plans,
preached the doctrine of civic unrest, led or followed
as was more effective, given of their time and money,
squandered their talents, urged people into the better
way of looking upon coöperative effort to improve
communal conditions.

The advertising man who is "worth his salt" has
got to see things moving. If he attends church, there
must be growth and progress or he loses interest. He
sets wheels in motion. If he plays golf on Sunday,
there is certain to be good golf and a good golf club.
He is moving all the time, and making others move.
He is usually working for betterment. Back of all his
business activity is the motive that seeks to better
business, better individuals, better the conditions of
trade, better the surroundings of the common man.
His sole claim for any business rests upon his assumed ability to make more trade and make better
trade. This underlying motive in advertising is its
donation to society. It is a sociological usufruct of
great value to society. No other class of business men
has the same character of impact upon society. No
other class has the same motives. None has the training, the instinct, or the ingrained tendency toward

the consideration of society in its coöperative capacity.

It is this demand of advertising upon the motor energies of the men immersed in it, and the results of this energetic constitutional promotion, that suggest to the investigating sociologist that there is a certain potentiality in advertising which is absent from other vocations, and which will prove to be a revolutionary force of no mean dimensions. Advertising, as a professional constituent of the social body, aside from its strict functions, has so profoundly influenced business methods and motives as to be entitled to credit for inciting to a true revolution. Whatever may truthfully be said of the *bona fides* of the motives that have led the mass of advertising men to join in the remarkable campaign for the square deal in business, typified by the shibboleth "Truth in Advertising," it is easily apparent that the sentiment as a practical working basis has spread into almost all the grand divisions of business.

It is now the fashion to insist upon fair play toward the consumers, it is known to be economic to look after the well-being of employés; whereas, a few years ago there was little heard about these sentimental attributes of business beyond the speeches at the conventions of the advertising men, they now posture as the most popular and engaging features of the conventions of other lines of business. It is nothing unusual to note that a great convention of hardware men, or electrical men, or druggists, or printers, or editors, has given its star assignments to

Social Effects

orators who play up sociological and humanitarian topics with all the fervor of their art, and the audiences that flock to listen are the largest and most enthusiastic of any at the sessions. At most of these conventions there are advertising men, and it is often that the trend of the conventions may be traced to their work and influence. The greatest of the experts who arrange conventions, manage them as a circus would be managed, are advertising men, accustomed to study and gauge the public. Formerly it was topics dealing with manufacture, distribution, or credits that were dealt with, with a mild spice of fraternalism that was expected to go no further than the grand banquet with which the meeting terminated. Now many of the subjects of addresses and discussions would be almost as apropos in a gathering of preachers or Sunday school superintendents.

Nothing can be more significant of the drawing together of business and ethics than this disposition of great class gatherings to tincture their deliberations with pure morality, real religion, or ideal altruism. And nothing is more indicative of the bent of advertising than the fact that this incursion of goodness into business is due to its initiative, though no advertising man will claim that all the credit is due to his confrères. While the profession of advertising has been the active agent for the spread of morality and altruism in business, it is quite content to note the returns and let who must have the credit.

But the real advertising man does not restrict his interest to social or religious phases of communal life. He promotes them because he must promote whatever he is interested in. He is interested in morality and religion because his psychological studies show him how necessary those are to the normal life. He is interested in all kinds of business because the promotion of business is his passion. He sees all kinds of business in terms of promotion. He cannot resist giving the hint that is needed. He analyzes every proposition he learns about, and in his mind formulates a plan to boost it. He knows conditions, and he mentally groups them around enterprises so that their activity may help the enterprises. He discovers and applies opportunity; often he creates opportunity. He dabbles in every industrial and mercantile enterprise in the town where he lives, and benefits them all. Many a suburban town or village or borough owes its life and prosperity to the ready initiative and inextinguishable energy of advertising men, who have given distinction and progress to their home communities with never a thought of reward.

The social product of the work of a live advertising man, or a well organized advertising agency, is much greater than the financial product. A good agency may promote some great business, like an automobile factory, and spend a million dollars a year in advertising it. The agency would receive something like $130,000 for its work, plus whatever might be charged for extra service. If the campaign was completely successful, a part of a prosperous business, the resulting business for the factory might be $20 000,000 to $25,000,000—not, of course, all due to advertising, but coming as the result of a general policy of which advertising was an important factor.

The social meaning of the spread of this business cannot be estimated. The advertising man who handled the advertising is to be credited with a large proportion of it. The moment an advertisement is printed, and begins to be read, the advertising man who made it begins to influence a widening circle of people, in some manner that would not otherwise have become operative.

Some guessers think that there are $600,000,000 spent every year in this country for advertising. Allow that 75 per cent of this sum is wasted—expended with so little wisdom or judgment that it has brought no return—there remains $150,000,000 that has been well spent. If it was spent on the basis of 5 per cent of gross receipts there would be a return of $3,000,000,000. If it had all been spent on a basis of 2 per cent for advertising, the gross business resulting from the business, making advertising one of the sales elements, would be $7,500,000,000. Advertising is not to be credited with all this income, but with its legitimate share. It has something vital to do with the getting of this great sum of money through advertising and other wise methods of selling. Just what proportion of this big sum it is fair to credit to advertising no man can tell.

Many of the great producing advertised businesses owe their existence to advertising, and all of their income, whether derived for any given year wholly from advertising or not, must be credited to advertising. This dalliance with large figures leads to the thought that all of the money brought into trade through advertising is the product of the brains of the advertising men, working in a sphere of business that is new, unique, different, and absolutely based upon the individual talents of the men who are in it.

Advertising methods are capable of a greater service to society than has been indicated. They will eventually form the basis for permanent policies which will operate to reform the processes of society in certain essential particulars. Thus far the students of publicity have limited their hopes to its temporary, or timely, effects. It is coming to be accepted that advertising may be employed to extinguish church debts, free a city from corruptionists, raise money for semi-public purposes, or in other directions assist in the accomplishment of good purposes. It is not yet much thought of in connection with fundamental plans for the permanent betterment of society, as a necessity in any plan that requires the coöperation of the people. For such purposes advertising must eventually be reckoned as one of the prime conditions.

Men's minds are slowly turning in this direction. The head of a great philanthropic · organization, when he sees that he must have a large sum of money, and considers that the usual methods for getting it are stale and have been overworked, thinks of advertising. The head of a big "foundation," established to turn people's minds into a certain channel, or furnish them with facilities they cannot hope to secure for

themselves, looks about for means to apply the benefits in his hands, and thinks of advertising. The great
church associations, wishing to appeal to the imagination of masses, think of advertising. Civic bodies
know that civic purity can be promoted better and
more quickly through advertising. Big financial deals
are easier handled with the help of advertising.

It is not an argument in rebuttal to say that these
great religious and philanthropic bodies have not yet
made great use of advertising. It is enough that they
are thinking of it. They will use it, and soon. They
must use it. There is no other method for getting
into touch with the people whose assistance they must
have. Advertising is a method of influencing people.
Preaching is also a method for influencing people.
The preacher may be able to move a larger proportion of his hearers than the advertiser can of his
readers. The preacher preaches to a handful of people—to from 50 to 500; rarely as many as 1,000;
and the man who is privileged to address 2,000 or
more on Sundays is very lonesome in the ministry. A
page advertisement judiciously inserted in the right
mediums may meet the eyes of five million people, or
ten million if the advertiser wishes—more people than
are addressed by all the ministers in the country.

In the days of the immediate future, when great
schemes in religion, sociology, government, and business, are contemplated, the vital question will be,
How can the minds of the people be so saturated with
this great motive as to make them willing to help?
There is but one reply: Make use of the methods of

advertising. Make advertising one of the fundamentals of the project, whatever it is, and through it make a sane and sound appeal to the people who ought to help. There is the great goal. It can only be reached through the help of many people. The only way to secure the help of many people is to appeal to many people; and there is no other sane and economic method of appealing to many people save advertising.

VIII

Church Advertising

In the field of religion advertising is destined to play a most important part.

Already it is being employed in the work of the more advanced churches and denominational organizations. There is a general sense, among the officials of the organizations and men who are brought intimately into contact with the world, and have to do with the business side of the churches, that the methods of promotion that have been accepted by business will have to be used by religious bodies. The disposition to advertise to attract attendance to the churches has grown very rapidly during the past ten years, and especially within the past two years. Progressive and ambitious preachers are making use of publicity methods to attract attendance, and there is a tentative feeling developing that larger mutual objects may be furthered by advertising.

The conception of the power and function of advertising is yet somewhat nebulous in the minds of those who are thinking of using it to further the ends of applied religion. They are using it to increase attendance at church meetings, and to induce people to give more service to the churches. This follows a fundamental error in the work of the religionists, and is in the nature of a reversal of the greatest potential power of advertising. A disposition to engage in the work of the churches is a by-product of religion. It is a mistake to employ advertising exclusively as a plea for the church, or as an incentive for church attendance. It means very little to ask the man who is not a church attendant to come to church. That is a question which he has settled for himself, and his determination not to attend church will not yield to moral urging to abandon it nor to pleas that the church needs him. He must be shown what the church offers him.

Advertising for the benefit of religion should be devoted to showing what the church has to offer to those who are not church people. In other words, the church must perfect its products and adopt a good sales policy. When it does so it can employ advertising to sell its goods.

Church advertising, so far as it has been developed, is too much in the nature of exhortation. If people will not go to the churches to be preached to it is not likely that preaching in advertisements will attract them. A sermon is a sermon, whether delivered from a pulpit in a church or through an advertisement in a newspaper. A collection of church advertisements gives one an impression similar to that received at the camp-meetings of our youth. The day for the argument that people must go to church to be saved has long passed. It is not effective. It is offensive, because it is not believed. It is rarely used in progressive pulpits. It should be absolutely barred from advertising the object of which is to promote the welfare of churches.

Here, perhaps, is the key to warranted criticism of advertising now being done in the name of religion:

Church Advertising

It is done for the welfare of the churches. The ordinary shrewd and sane person, who is not a church person, believes that the church is an expression of the religious ideas of the people who constitute it, and not in any sense an authoritative expression of religion. He does not assent to the proposition that churches are essential to religion, and that neglect of the churches is tantamount to a rejection of religion. He feels no sense of a personal, religious obligation to support, or to attend, any church. He is not, in his own conscience, convicted of sin if he altogether neglects the churches. The man who plays golf on Sundays does not feel that he is therefore a sinner. This attitude toward the churches may be right or wrong. It exists. Advertising is not a court of morals. It is a method of persuading people.

In its scheme for advertising for its own benefit the church must take account of the state of mind in which it finds the people it wishes to win. It must take account of its own condition, and the causes that have led to its condition. That it has lost the security of its hold upon the people is the cause of its greatest anxiety, and, if it stops to reflect, it can scarcely hope to win them back to the old implicit allegiance simply through urging them to again attach themselves to its organizations. It must show its goods, and show that they are such as will benefit and please the people. The church is no longer the *summum bonum* of the spiritual life of the thinking people. It is only one avenue for the expression of their spirituality, and not even an essential one. Ardent church people dispute this. But it is not their conception of the church that needs to be impressed upon those who do not attend church. It is the conception of the outsider that has to be considered as the foundation of the advertising motive.

To succeed in an advertising campaign in behalf of the churches it is necessary that the churches shall project themselves into the lives of those they wish to attract. It is of little use for them to exploit themselves, attempt to show what they are and what they offer. They must do more than offer their goods: they must shrewdly promote their acceptance—their sale, if we may continue to make use of the terminology of trade. A church may open its doors never so wide, and expose its interior with all possible fidelity—it has still to go out and get its converts on their own grounds. It cannot ask people to come to it, as a chief advertising motive—it must go to them. When a person is convinced that the church has something of benefit to him, he will go to it, but he will not go to it simply because the church wishes to have him, or needs him ever so badly.

The first essential for effective church advertising is therefore that the church neglect itself and its necessities and devote its energies to studying the attitude of those it seeks to attract, and to showing them what it has to offer them that they need. That the church needs them should be forgotten, in the initial stages of the campaign at least, and only made use of in the cases of individuals who acknowledge their need of the church but withhold their personal

WHY NOT GO TO CHURCH?

Few persons think things through. If everybody reasoned this matter of church-going to its logical conclusion there would not be many vacant pews, and a widespread demand for more churches would speedily arise.

The reason is simple: People do not stay away from church because they are opposed to religion or to the Church. Far from it. Nearly, everybody believes that the Christian Church is absolutely necessary to our civilization. If its existence were threatened, the great mass of the people would fight for it.

But by some curious kink in their mental processes, many non-church-goers fail to perceive that if everybody else followed their example — and every honest **person grants others the right to do as he does** — the churches would quickly pass out of existence.

Every non-attendant upon religious services virtually votes for the elimination of the institution from society. If a person believes that the world needs the Church, he has but one clear, unmistakable and unanswerable way of stating his position. That is by regular church attendance. The man who goes to church stands for an indispensable institution, even as a good citizen stands for the state by voting.

In Case of Illness, Death or Other Trouble, Any Minister Will Be Glad to Help.

Absenteeism from the ballot-box and absenteeism from church are kindred failures in duty to society. Of course that is not the best reason for church attendance. We go to church primarily to express our belief in God and to do Him reverence. The loftiest truth about man is that he is made in the image of the Divine and has a capacity for fellowship with the Infinite. Worship is the highest function of which human nature is capable.

The world does not know much about creeds, but when it sees a person attending divine worship it understands him to say by his action, "I believe in God."

Thoughtful persons stand for the Church, also because **the Church stands for the best things.** The church-goer lines up with the forces which make for righteousness. He is on the side of the people who want to live the noblest lives themselves and who are trying to help this needy world to do the same.

The most efficient agency of human service on earth is the Christian Church. The churchman is a sharer in all the world-wide beneficence of the organization.

They who would make their lives count should be counted among those upon whom the Church may count.

[115]

An effective Church Advertisement, occupying about one-third of a newspaper page.

coöperation. Advertising for religion must proceed along the lines that have been proved profitable for business. It is the old, worn, vague shibboleths of religion that have weaned people from the churches. It is useless to repeat them in advertising and hope for satisfactory results.

When the churches, and all the interests of religion, get the right viewpoint for their advertising, the advertising profession will assure them that they command a field from the proper cultivation of which may be expected to flow results that will revolutionize the spiritual life of the world.

Spiritual aspiration is a human attribute that is assuming greater importance and significance with each generation. Our sons and daughters accept into their lives certain fundamental propositions relating them to a higher spiritual life than we dared hope for, quite irrespective of their church affiliations, or non-affiliations. They are more susceptible to spiritual suggestion than we were, notwithstanding that we were under the domination of a strict church-going régime. We were anxious about manifestations; they do not give those manifestations a thought. We thought of the inner spirit with awe, and some doubt; they are as confident of its control as of the rising of the sun, and as unconscious of doubt regarding it. They are ready for suggestions that involve expression and service. They do not care for form, for tradition, for assumption, for allegations regarding religion that make of it something extraneous to their ordered and ascertained lives.

Church Advertising

This present generation of people who are earnest in their present attitude toward life constitutes the best material for the churches they have ever been able to contemplate. Much of it is now cool in its church interest. A too large proportion is hostile. These people will not respond to mere requests to attend church, or to assist churches as now organized. Yet they are as ductile as clay in the hands of the potter. They yearn for opportunities for work along lines leading manifestly to the betterment of the race, the improvement of the times. This is, they believe, salvation. They are ready to join any organization that promises them work, scope, room for growth, enlarged vision, uplift, satisfaction for that passion for helping others that is in every ardent heart.

To such people the churches have only to say, "Come and work in this field with us," and they will come; only the field must be specified, and the methods of work clearly outlined. These points assured, the modern enthusiasts who have kept away from the churches because the churches were too cold will not care whether it is the church or another organization that beckons them. The times are ripe for the greatest revival of religion the world has ever seen. It will not come through the old church channels, and so long as the invitation is to use those old channels the great revival will hesitate. Nothing is needed now but that the churches see the vision, adapt themselves, and inaugurate the greatest advertising campaign ever conceived.

This translation of the dream of Armageddon into

terms of persuasion for the people, the leading them
into the better life, the making of religion the popular element of sane life that it was meant to be, is the
great dream of advertising men who realize the
power of their profession and the needs of mankind.
It is a problem easier of solution than those dealt
with every day. It involves nothing in the way of
payment or sacrifice. It is, on the part of the people,
all receiving, and receiving something they had been
wishing for, hungering for, hoping for. That this
great thing is not pressed upon the people with all
the vigor employed in the great commercial advertising campaigns is due only to the constitutional slow-
ness of mankind to reach out and take benefits that
are always being offered; and to the clinging of the
churches to the past.

Suppose the series of advertisements the size of a
standard magazine page were to be made, twelve for
the monthlies, fifty-two for the weeklies, and 365 for
the dailies, stating the benefits of religion in terms
of those people who care nothing for the churches,
and printed in leading publications for a year. What
would be the effect? Suppose that the effect of these
advertisements was carefully watched by a competent corps of experts, and every necessary follow-up
was employed. Suppose that all of the preachers were
to agree to work along the same lines for a year—
not preach from the same texts nor in the same vein,
but devote themselves for the year to the task of
bringing religion into the lives of the people through
the natural channels, along lines of the least resist-

ance and without reference to theology. Suppose that this entire campaign were to be planned in coöperation with a board of the best advertising men, the best sociologists, the best psychologists, the best preachers, the best laymen—a board of 100 men, working through sub-committees, and giving a month to program-making.

This would be a campaign for religion such as the world has never seen, and the results would be such as would set religion further in advance than the usual methods would put it in a generation. Would it not be worth while? What would it cost? Not one per cent of the returns. It would be the cheapest, most economical method possible to imagine. It would tremendously reduce crime and immorality. It is perfectly feasible. There is money enough available. It would not cost so very much, compared with other great social movements. It would be the sanest and most business-like thing the churches could do. It would make America the greatest nation in the world. It would promote religion all over the world. The people are ready. Where is the great leader who will marshal the churches and the laymen? There are in the ranks of the advertising men a dozen, any of whom could be the generalissimo. There are among the men of great wealth plenty who can, and would, finance it. All of the periodicals would help. Many of them would give the space for the advertising. The newspapers would give the plan publicity.

Is it a dream? If it is, it is such a dream as advertising men have. They are the true evangels of the times. Let the churches turn to them. They can make religion popular. The churches have not succeeded in doing it, and unless they change their point of view they will not. That they are turning to the advertising men is a very hopeful sign. That they are thinking of advertising as one of their ordinary functions is not in itself so hopeful. This conception of the power of advertising is a part of the lives of advertising men. It is practically impossible that others share it. Others do not know what advertising is or what it can do. The supreme aspiration of the genuine advertising man is that some day he may have an opportunity to apply advertising to some great social or religious object, and religious promoters are making the mistake of not turning their advertising plans over to the zealous advertising men. The fault with current religious advertising is that there is too much religion in it, and not enough advertising skill.

There has been growing up, during the past few years, a body of evidence as to the efficiency of advertising for religious promotion that is getting to be very convincing and conclusive, notwithstanding the handicap of lack of professional advertising knowledge and skill. It has always had a strong human-interest appeal, and wherever it has been done with anything like continuity and persistence it has shown excellent results. It has not yet got a very firm hold on the imagination of the church people. Most of them look upon it as undignified or insincere. It is considered to be unethical, but for what reason it is impossible to imagine. Dentists and doctors do not

Church Advertising

consider it professional to advertise, and lawyers profess to be of the same mind. Ministers are ranked as in the pale of professionalism, and they are therefore expected to agree with the professional traditions.

But there are ministers who believe in advertising, and try to practice it. Some of their efforts are creditable, but if the existing church advertising were to be compared with advertising by commercial interests it would sink to third rate, or below. There are notable exceptions. There is a Methodist minister in New York who not only advertises his church, but has written an interesting book about "Church Publicity." It is a very notable book, from the fact of its existence and its origin. It is a unique book. It does not deal with advertising *per se.* The author, Rev. Christian F. Reisner, sent out to a list of ministers an elaborate questionaire, covering every aspect of church publicity, and he has built this book around the letters he received, using his questions to the ministers as chapter topics, interlarding the quotations with pithy comments, and closing each chapter with a statement of his own conclusions. The book is sprinkled with reproduced advertisements, and there are many quotations from other books on advertising, and letters from advertising men. It is a case book, full of detail and reports. The author does not attempt to relate advertising to religion except as a means for attracting people to the churches, nor does he interest himself with the philosophy of advertising. He accepts it as a more or less organized method of hustling for more attendance in the churches, and justifies its use by the results it has in that line shown.

There have been several other good books written about church advertising, the most notable being by Rev. Charles Stelzle, "Principles of Successful Church Advertising." Mr. Stelzle does not show that the principles of advertising that are to be employed to promote a church are different from those employed to promote a dry-goods store, as of course they are not; but he does strike the right note in defining what should be the attitude of the church toward its promotion. "The point is," he remarks, "to make men see that the church, as it is organized, governed, and attempting to help men toward God and to fulfil their duty toward their fellows, is the best organization with which they may become affiliated." This admirable sentiment is followed by the remark that "the church should advertise because men must be reached where they are." This is more in the nature of a textbook, after the proposition that churches should advertise had been demonstrated, and its suggestions are along the lines of good advertising practice.

While it is to be said that the churches are none too forward in their acceptance of advertising as the most efficient aid they can invoke, it is evident that advertising will be accepted as the greatest force for the promotion of religion.

IX

Efficient Advertising

Is advertising, as it is now practiced, efficient?

Advertising as it is now practiced is not efficient, if the standards of efficiency in other phases of business are to be used in judging it.

Some advertising is extremely efficient. Everybody knows that advertising has created great businesses. It is no romance to say that there are many big fortunes, many very big businesses, that owe their being to advertising. The tale of the Down East Yankee who risked his last dollars to pay for a half-inch advertisement in several periodicals, offering to do something about which he knew practically nothing, and to sell something that was not then in existence, and his subsequent great business and big fortune, is familiar—and it is typically true. The tale of the man in the West who had changed his last five-dollar bill when in sheer desperation he wrote a little advertisement offering to teach young men a certain business process, and thus started one of the most successful and money-making of those recent instruction schools, is also typical. A patent-medicine man died recently, leaving a fortune of more than five millions, all made through advertising, and advertising that never did anybody the smallest bit of good. Instances of money made by advertising may be multiplied, beyond the limits of a five-foot shelf of books, and at the end of the list we would

Advertising

have sadly to confess that a list of the failures due to unwise and ignorant advertising would fill volumes enough for a twenty-foot shelf. Every well-informed advertising man can relate instances of great advertising successes, and when he shall have emptied himself of his facts, he will admit, with reluctance and chagrin, that for every success he is able to cite he can recall three or four failures. It is loosely said that as much as 75 per cent of advertising current in any year disappears from the mediums by the next year. This percentage is, it is fondly believed, growing less; so that when these hazy approximations are being read the percentage of disappearances for that year may have declined to 70, or even to 65, per cent.

Why is it that advertising—that business element which is believed to rest upon scientific principles easily known and readily put into practice—is so inefficient? It is a fair question, and ought to be answered clearly and categorically. The trouble is that the answer is so simple that it is hard to believe it is all the answer that is required. More advertisers insist upon advertising wrongly than are willing to advertise rightly. That is all there is to the answer, only it is one of those answers that do not answer.

Advertising in the modern sense is new. There are few professional advertising men. There were none at all until very recently. Those who are now more or less entitled to the distinction are not all-round advertising professors. They are narrow, and, while equipped to originate a successful campaign in one direction, have limitations that assure failure in

others. They all make one or more successes, and
more than one or more failures. Each of their failures
contributes to that large percentage in the field.
But if the professional advertising men made all the
failures the percentage of success in the general field
would be very much larger. The lamentable failures
in advertising are made by the men who have to find
the money to finance the failures. The idea prevailing among many of the smaller advertisers is that
the writing and placing of the advertisements is work
that any clerk, or even the proprietor, can do when
there is nothing else to be done, like washing the
office windows or drawing checks. Who should know
so much about the right advertising for a concern
as the man who owns it, built it up, and manages
it? This man says: "Can an outsider come in here
and tell me about my business?" Then he takes a
pencil and writes an advertisement, which has nine
chances to one against it being anything but a flat
failure. The man writes to himself.

Advertising has been unsuccessful also because it
has so often been employed to promote impossible
propositions, and propositions that were not formulated to win. There was once a manufacturing concern that had prepared for the market an entirely
new thing in the fabric line, and had also prepared
an advertising campaign, with the assistance of an
agent. The agent called upon the manager of the
leading trade paper in that line, and proposed to
make a large contract with him. This man knew the
art of advertising, and insisted upon knowing all

about the new material, its manufacture, and the plans for selling. After he had got all this information he declined to publish the advertising. The agent and the manufacturer pleaded with him in vain. Pressed to give reasons, he told the manufacturer that the fabric was not adapted for the market, and that his plans for selling and advertising were not well considered; and he took the trouble to explain. The manufacturer saw that the publisher was right, and the campaign was abandoned. The fabric was radically changed, the manufacturing plans were modified in accordance with the suggestions of the publisher, and the selling and advertising plans were remodeled. Then the publisher accepted the advertising, and the fabric became very popular and profitable. The publisher claimed none of the credit, took no fee, turned the advertising campaign over to the agent who first appeared in the defective plans, and got no more advertising for his paper than he would have had if he had not taken the pains to nip the foredoomed scheme in the bud. This sort of practical service is not offered by all periodicals, and will not be accepted by many advertisers. This man happened to be an authority whose opinion could not be disputed, and the periodical happened to be the one that was absolutely needful.

The reason for the failure of much of the advertising is that it is so crudely done. When there are advertising experts, in the true sense, and when advertisers realize that advertising is not the same as making goods, nor the same as selling them, but is absolutely the work of the man who knows advertising, there will be less inefficient advertising. There will always be much advertising that will produce nothing but failure, because it is so often employed to promote gambles. It will be necessary to imagine that advertising will always be done for genuine enterprises, as well as that it will be expertly done, to even conceive that it will be more than from 30 to 40 per cent efficient. If advertising as a whole were now 40 per cent efficient, advertising men would consider that the millennium was at hand.

The mediums contribute their full share to the inefficiency of advertising. So many of them are eager to sell space that they do not discriminate. When publishers all act in the common-sense and helpful manner of the one here quoted there will be much less ineffective advertising. When all the advertising used is well conceived and properly written and displayed, there will be less ineffective advertising. When merchants and manufacturers cease trying to sell unmarketable goods through advertising, there will be less ineffective advertising. When all the elements that go to the making of effective advertising are applied to all the advertising, then there will be a record for advertising that will show near to 100 per cent efficiency.

There is now probably about as great a percentage of industrial failure brought about through other commercial lesions as through bad advertising, but these failures have been happening always and do not cause remark. Nevertheless, advertising should not be inclined to plead this sort of a demurrer, and is not so inclined. It is now quite possible for the advertiser who is as shrewd and liberal in his publicity as in his manufacturing and merchandizing to predicate the results of his advertising. It is as certain as the sale of goods that have not yet been manufactured, or as any of the prime elements of business that have to be reckoned with. Given the goods, the people to be converted into customers, and the skilful advertising man, there is little danger that the campaign will take its place among the failures. It is one of the surest things in business.

There is a certain style, if it may be so called, that is almost always successful. It is where the business and the man who does the advertising are so closely related as to give a basis for thorough knowledge, and where the man who knows the business is permitted to do the advertising. There are some scores, or possibly hundreds, of concerns that have always done successful advertising, and whose advertising has been done by the same men for years. These advertising men are not what one would call advertising experts. They might not succeed if called upon to change their venue. But they know the businesses that they have promoted so well that their work has become an integral part of those enterprises. They are more than advertising managers. They usually have something vital to do with the selling department, and not infrequently they are officials of their corporations with influence in the manufac-

turing and general business departments. They have
studied their problems for many years. They have
traveled among the customers of their houses. They
have met the retailers that handle their goods. They
personally know the traveling salesmen. They work
with the sales managers. The business of these concerns has been worked into the blood of these advertising men. They have learned to know how to appeal
to the people who use their goods. They know how
to select mediums, and what forms of advertising
are adapted to their needs. They go about their work
with the sure touch of complete knowledge. They
are advertising managers who advertise. There is no
guesswork with them. They do not know what inefficient advertising is. They are not dominated by
officials who do not know but are bound to rule. They
know how to combat their superiors, as well as how
to bring into line a serviceable publisher. They have
their fingers upon the pulse of the readers of all the
periodicals they use, and they know just what product to offer through this or that magazine or newspaper, and just how to offer it. Such ingrained ex-
pertness cannot be attained by the advertising man
who has to deal with many problems, or who has to
deal with one problem as men over him dictate. It
is, perhaps, a condition of the greater efficiency of
advertising that it shall be dealt with by men who
spend their lives specializing with one advertiser.
Perhaps advertising is that sort of a profession that
demands of each practitioner that he specialize, that
his work be so intensive as to leave nothing in his

restricted field to be referred to general principles, or described in general terms.

The efficiency of advertising depends, it seems, upon the *bona fides* of the advertised offer, upon the *bona fides* of the concern making the offer, the quality of the thing offered, the skill and freedom of the man who actually does the advertising. It depends upon the human elements in the problem—the human need for the goods, the human spirit of the offer of the goods, the qualities of the person transmitting the offer to the potential buyers. It is a matter of man to man.

These elements of advertising efficiency are more or less under the control of the advertiser. He can, if he knows how and is skilful, adjust them to the exigencies of the problem he has to deal with. He can adjust his goods to the needs of the people who are within the scope of his distribution scheme and the capacity of his production facilities. He can be honest in intention and practice, and he can make honest goods and advertise them truthfully. But he still has the great problem of his appeal to the people he must interest to deal with—his selection of his advertising mediums. This is one of the more perplexing of all the problems connected with the efficiency of advertising. It causes the most study, much of the study being almost fruitless because there is such a lack of knowledge of their publications by publishers. For the most part advertisers have to rely upon their own judgment and investigations to furnish them data relative to the efficiency of advertising mediums, and even with respect to the raw facts upon which some estimate of efficiency can be based. With full knowledge of the mediums, the problem is still very difficult.

Sales and advertising managers have attempted to arrive at some approximate estimate of the efficiency of their advertising, but have always to begin with assumptions, and usually to end with results based almost as much upon guesswork as upon demonstrated facts. One assumes, for example, that 25 per cent of the readers of a certain periodical may be interested in goods to be advertised, because he thinks that not more than that proportion of the general class of people he understands read that periodical could economically use the goods. Of this 25 per cent he discovered, through his system of keying, that only 10 per cent seemed actually to be interested in his advertising. This meant that only 2.5 per cent of the readers of the periodical were available to him as "prospects." His actual sales inquiries (not sales) were but 10 per cent of this 2.5 per cent, or one-fourth of 1 per cent of the circulation of the periodical. Suppose that the periodical has 200,000 circulation, there are but 500 of its readers who will buy the goods of this advertiser. How much money will these 500 sales bring in, and how much profit, and what relation is there between this profit and the cost of the advertising?

Such an analysis of the cost of advertising is not satisfactory, nor conclusive. It leaves some of the vital elements out of the account, and the result is

not all to be charged to advertising. The efficiency
of advertising is seriously affected by some elements
that are usually reckoned to be quite outside of
advertising. The advertising and the selling are firmly linked together. Trade conditions vitally influence
the efficiency of advertising. The distribution plans
affect the result of advertising. The character of the
goods fixes the first element in assessing efficiency.
Social economic movements, and faddism, in respect
to some of the departments of practical living, may
make certain lines of advertising efficient or almost
useless, for the time being. The agitation for pure
food and drugs, the coming of the "hobble" skirts
for women, the fashion for big hats, and like social
and economic phenomena, affect advertising. No
manufacturer of women's wear would hope to make
advertising of petticoats profitable while women wear
skirts like the leg of a man's trousers.

Bringing the element of good faith into advertising is working a momentous change. People are getting wise in this business, as in others, and are beginning to apply sophisticated reasoning to their response to advertising. Any estimate of the efficiency
of advertising must take account of the swing from
dishonest to honest advertising that is going on. It
is a most salutary movement, but it disturbs equilib-
rium, and makes it difficult to predicate.

There is an ideal conception of advertising efficiency. If the product advertised is a staple which
is used in every family, or by every individual, like
soap, and the advertiser offers a variety of qualities

so that he can claim that he can economically make all the soap for all the people who read the periodical in which he advertises, he can claim that his goods have 100 per cent of advertising potentiality. If his advertising copy was to be so written that it appealed with equal force to every reader of the periodical who looked at the advertising section, and had sufficient appeal to move all who read it to buy, he might assume that his advertising was 100 per cent efficient. But even so he would not know what proportion of the readers were interested in the advertising pages, and it would be exceedingly difficult to find out. Yet, given these ideal advertising conditions, and equal conditions applying to production, selling, distribution, and general business policy, there would result ideal advertising efficiency—whatever that might mean for different propositions.

If such an advertising proposition were possible, there would be an element to deal with which would make all the other elements uncertain in their operation toward that ideal 100 per cent efficiency. The advertisee may be all that he should be in the way of interest and potential need, yet he may not be a buyer; and why he may not buy is an element of mystery that it is quite impossible to solve. Habit has made him a customer of the local stores, and they do not choose to stock the article advertised. He may for the time being be supplied with another brand, and, despite his conviction that the advertised article is better, he will use the stock on hand—and very likely renew it when it is exhausted. The flow of habit cannot at once be checked by an advertisement, or other means. A man continues to do that which he has been doing, and is unable to explain why he does it. If all the people who are intellectually convinced by advertising bought advertised goods advertising would be 100 per cent more efficient than it now is. The great problem is to induce people to do that which they know they ought to do, or would profit through doing. The reason that no advertisement that is theoretically 100 per cent efficient is ever half, or a quarter, as efficient in actual practice is that people do not do as they ought. Of course, one should yield to the demands of the advertisements, if convinced that it would be well to do so. People should do that, in all relations of life, which they know is best for them to do. They do not, and because they do not there is the wide gap between theoretical and actual advertising efficiency.

Another difficulty is that advertising conditions are not well known, and that there is no real effort afoot to make them well known; they have not been subject to careful and scientific analysis, from the standpoint of the publisher or of the advertiser. The mediums do not, as a general proposition, know what it is they are offering when they invite advertisers to use their pages. They think of the problem in terms of figures on their ledgers. They know a little about their readers, but not enough to enable them to advise advertisers as to the degree of efficiency they can assure them. They assert that they print and distribute so many copies, but they do not know how many of those people actually read their periodicals, or in what spirit they read them. Least of all do they know how many of their subscribers read the advertisements they print, or what would induce them to read more. They do not know how their readers look upon the advertising printed, in a general sense. They have never taken measures to find out. They are, most of them, afraid to do so, being conscious of a certain dumb hostility to the advertisements among their readers, so far as anything in that line has ever come to them. They have never thought much about making their periodicals readable, thinking of the reading matter only, and they are quite helpless when it comes to making their readers turn to the advertising for profit or entertainment. Depending upon the advertising for their revenue, publishers do very little to make the advertising interesting to their readers, and so profitable to their advertisers.

There lies here, in coöperation between the publishers and the advertisers, a great field now measurably unworked, the proper cultivation of which may be made to render advertising much more efficient, and all to the pleasure and benefit of the readers also. It is for the publisher to see that the right appeal is made to his readers, and it is for him to know his readers well enough to show him what that appeal must be. It is for the publisher to gather the audience for the advertiser, and also to study the psychology of the audience for the advertiser.

X

The Advertising Man

So we come through these main avenues of approach to the vital element in advertising—that which makes of it one of the more exalted professions of this twentieth century, and justifies all the attention that is being given it.

How does this profession, that puts its finger upon the motor nerve of man, affect the men who are engaged in it, and how is it to affect the general question of the relations of men to one another?

Advertising rests upon the good faith of one man, exercised to influence the lives and happiness of other men. Advertising is selling "unsight unseen." The advertiser makes certain statements in a manner and fashion to secure the faith and credence of other men who read the advertisements. There is no opportunity for the readers to test the quality of the statements made by the advertiser. There is sometimes a weak provision that goods may be returned, or some other attempt to persuade the reader that his interests are considered. They are not otherwise protected than through the word of the advertiser. If he tells the truth—if he is inclined to give a square deal—the buyer need not beware. If he is not thus inclined, if he considers that all the readers who rely upon his statements are therefore fair game, there is little hope for the advertiser who is inclined to keep his faith in his kind.

The Advertising Man

In most of the business of life the buyer has a chance to exercise his judgment, and if he makes mistakes there is not the same quality of turpitude to be charged to the seller as to the advertiser who lies in his advertisements. The persons who read advertising have no defense against the arguments there made use of. This is the challenge to the advertiser, and it is this that separates advertising morality from the ordinary variety of business efforts. There is a certain stimulus in the doctrine of Caveat Emptor, as applied to transactions between persons, because the buyer is then able to see the thing offered and appraise the personality of the seller. If he gets defrauded he is, to a degree, responsible.

We are inclined to believe everything we read, in advertising, in news, and other literature. We have much to say about the unreliability of newspapers, yet we believe, without questioning, more than 99 per cent of all we read in them. That item we doubt is something that we happen to know about, or have an opinion about which is different from the interpretation the newspaper has given it. Our faith is automatic. It is one of the subtleties of our mental being that we believe whatever we are told. If we disbelieve we must make a distinct effort to formulate the doubt, and we have to exercise the will to get it recognized by our minds. We are constituted, by that Power which has created the earth and man to possess it, to accept what is told us. Our minds are made to work that way. The motor principle, as it is called, works affirmatively.

Advertising

We are mental sponges, and absorb whatever is poured out upon us, by advertisers and others. If it were in our human nature to observe and analyze the allegations of the advertisers, and balance one probability against another in coming to a conclusion about that statement, we could protect ourselves. We cannot do that. All of our mental pores are open to receive affirmatively whatever comes to us. Doubt is unnatural; not only unnatural in its essence, but practically impossible with respect to a large percentage of the suggestions that come to us. We never doubt without having a good reason for the doubt. It is the natural method of the mind to say *yes* to every request—to do whatever asked to do. The whole world moves upon this principle—the principle of doing whatever seems right to do, or whatever some one asks us to do. When we begin to cultivate doubt, when we refuse to respond, when we debate and hesitate, we begin to retrograde. The man who is a habitual doubter speedily segregates himself, and his fellows pass him by.

The shrewd advertiser knows this motor principle of the mind, and counts upon it to help him sell his goods. He knows that if he can make the right appeal, and can get his appeal within the conscious range of the reader's vision, he can sell the things he has for sale. He knows that people are almost helpless in his hands, if he can get them to realize that he is speaking to them. The question of the efficacy of advertising is simpler than it is understood to be. It hinges upon getting the attention of people in a pleasing manner. The attention power possessed by people who read any one periodical is usually far too limited to take note of all the advertising offered. There is only a certain proportion of readers who will submit themselves to the temptation of the advertisements, and but a very small proportion who make a careful survey of the advertising pages of their favorite magazines or their morning and evening newspapers. The normal buying power of the readers of any large periodical is many hundred times greater than the most phenomenal returns any advertising ever gets. The total returns received by any advertiser are to be reckoned as one to 1,000 of that which he might receive if all the readers of his mediums who should fairly be interested in his proposition were in fact interested in it.

Running through all these advertising methods and manifestations is the golden thread of personal responsibility—the man-to-man basic idea—accepted as a rule of conduct by more and more advertising men each year. When their peculiar responsibility becomes quite clear to advertising men it takes a firmer hold of their consciousness than do many of the more obvious and usual bases of conduct. He is very much of a brute who will take advantage of the trust of a child. The trust that a reader of advertisements must have is like the trust of the child, who does not know that there is such a thing as deceit in the world. The readers of advertisements know that there is deceit in some of them, but the conditions of their being make it impossible to know that there is deceit in any particular advertisement. So it has come about that the really big advertising man is getting to be a really honest man, and so it is that we are bound to indorse all we hear about truth in advertising, in the hope that the men who have suddenly become so vociferous mean all they say.

The new move for honest advertising is having a marked effect upon business. It is rapidly sweeping chicane and subterfuge off their feet. It is demonstrating that truth is the best selling maxim; which has a certain sordid suggestion, but it is surely better to be fair even if that is the road leading to the greatest possible profits.

In this one great branch of business the men have come to a new and different plane of associational life. It is but a few years since any advertising man would think of treating another advertising man with frankness and openness. Now they treat each other with the utmost openness. Nothing in the way of trade secrets is reserved. Nothing in the way of fellowship is omitted. Brotherhood, in its truest sense, has entered into this business. It is in evidence in all lines, though it is the proud belief of advertising men that they have led the way, promoted the movement and put it first into their own practices.

The student of sociological conditions has noted that in all branches of business the personal equation is coming to be more esteemed; that there is brotherhood among the men engaged in identical pursuits. This drawing together of the social man and the business man is one of the significant signs of the times. Exactly what it signifies we are not yet able to estimate. That it is to be a wonderful emollient for the civilization we hope for is evident.

Perhaps it is too much to claim that this movement became first manifest through the remarkable club movement among advertising men, but it is certain that they were in the forefront of the wave of brotherhood in business. It is only about five years since the formation of clubs of advertising men became notable, and now there are not less than 12,000 men enrolled in some 300 clubs throughout the United States. These clubs have a national organization called the Associated Advertising Clubs of the World, the annual conventions of which have become the greatest inspirational meetings held anywhere in the world, considering the character of the motives that are back of the whole movement—strictly business motives. These conventions have, for four years, given themselves, with true camp-meeting abandon, to the propagation of the simple fundamental proposition that advertising should not lend itself to schemes that tend to degrade or defraud. These advertising men have discovered that it is more profitable, in the long run, to treat people fairly, and it seems that this discovery appeals to them as so new and novel as to make them evangels of commerce, apostles of the newer dispensation of business, prophets of that ideal altruism we all hope will some day be as effectual in business as in social or religious life.

In whatever wise we look at advertising we see that

it, so far as it is done in the light of its newer ideals,
tends to lift and clarify social conditions and make
the traffic between individuals more frank and
brotherly. If we are satisfied that it does these things,
and that it is also the great business force its students and advocates claim, it seems that advertising
is one of our twentieth century causes for thanks-
giving. That it is, in its essence, a challenge to good
faith, and that it compels a self-respecting man to
respect his neighbor as himself, is the fundamental
human base of advertising that lifts it above ordinary
business and differentiates it from ordinary social
motives. That the essential attributes of the best
advertising involve almost all of the virtues specified
by the Decalogue, bearing upon the intercourse of
people, while at the same time absorbing those attributes of successful business that are most essential, implies that it may be considered somewhat in
the light of a connecting link to ultimately draw
them much closer together. Its influence in this direction is already discoverable in the minds of its more
enthusiastic students and apologists; and they are
able to make out a very good case.

In no other business is there such incentive to do
wrong and such opportunity for doing good. The
advertising man is obliged to depend upon his ability
to move people. He is subject to the temptation to
exert his influence for his exclusive benefit. To turn
the back upon an opportunity for personal benefit
is one of the hardest things in the world to do. The
advertising man is always having to decide between

The Advertising Man

the other man and himself. His responsibility is a
very different thing from the general responsibility
we all share for all others. There is always for him
in view some dollars that he feels sure he can get, if
he is willing to forget that he is his brother's keeper.
It is because so many do forget this that advertising
has such a clouded reputation. When there are dollars
in sight, within reach, it is only the true man who
turns his back on them because of his regard for the
man who is ready, and perhaps anxious, to deliver
them up.

The difference between advertisers is that one class
are content to use advertising as one method of promoting legitimate business, and the other class use it
for getting money. The Louisiana lottery was a
method of getting money, and it employed many of
the usages and forms of fairness and honesty, but
it was a piratical enterprise and in time public sentiment made it impossible. Its managers did not conceal
from its dupes the fact that nearly all of them would
lose their money. What it emphasized was that a few
of them would get some of the money that the many
lost. Fraudulent advertising is like the Louisiana
lottery—the advertisers can only gain through the
loss of those who respond to the advertising. It is
surer than burglary, though no more reputable or
justifiable. There are delicate and subtle moral
nuances in advertising. The advertisement of a
strictly legitimate article, offered by a reputable
concern, may be made as immoral and deceptive as
the advertisements of the Louisiana lottery.

Advertising

There is a very vital difference between the advertising lure and the advertising bait. The lure we must use, the bait we should not use. That advertising man who will consciously use the bait is immoral, no matter who are his principals or what is the article he is advertising.

Ready money is so to be desired. Trade is so necessary. There is such a resolve in business to secure quick results that the advertising man feels that he must yield to it. He must often yield to it or sacrifice himself and those dependent upon him. Success means money in hand to so many business men that the advertising man considers he must play for it. Every good advertising man knows that the best advertising works for the future, tends to implant in people's minds the idea that will blossom into trade in its own good time, and will continue to bring forth the fruit of profit. But they also know that there must be immediate results. They do not have a choice. They have got to work for the order of to-morrow. Therefore are they tempted to make use of the illegitimate assertion, the warped phrase, the exaggerated description, the deceptive tendency.

It may be pleaded that something must be allowed for attractive power, and something left for the discretion of the buyer. Not in legitimate advertising, because there is no opportunity for reaction in advertising. The party of the other side cannot take part in the arrangement of the deal that is being framed up against him. The reader of the advertisement must answer its appeal with a *yes* or a *no*. It is

The Advertising Man

not possible for him to consider, to get more information, to ask questions, to demand tests and proofs. The advertisement is inarticulate along those lines. It cannot discuss—it can only assert. If therefore the advertiser does other than to present his case in impeccable, unvarnished, and naked truth he is guilty of deceit—the same quality of deceit employed by the sneak who steals pennies from the blind man's cup. The smudge on character because of deceptive advertising is blacker than that bestowed by other varieties of larceny, because the victim cannot resist.

There are many advertising men who do not yield to the temptation to deceive in their work. Most of these are poor. They are big men, nevertheless, and their ranks are filling up. While the deceptive advertising man is a particularly despicable person, the straight and honest one is an especially fine specimen of commercial manhood.

In other ways beside honesty advertising men are remarkable, because of the business they are in. They are broad-minded, because that type of man attracts and can influence his fellows. They come to be very accomplished, and to be wells of erudition and knowledge. What the trained and seasoned advertising man does not come to know, and know about, is so obscure as to be of little interest. If he stays in one line, he becomes an accomplished expert in that line. If he is a general practitioner, he becomes an expert in many lines and cultivates a capacity for absorbing knowledge. He is prone to be a student of psychology, which leads into the pleasantest paths of science and life. He must become an expert sociologist, which puts him in touch with the quality and character of people and makes him a brother of humanity. These two branches of humanity he must study and understand. His most notable accomplishment must be his touch upon his fellows, leading to much that is broadening, deepening, uplifting and delightful, apart from professional utility.

The real advertising man is oil upon the troubled waters of business and social life. He learns how to impress himself upon his associates without risking reaction. He trains his spirit to give and never think of a return. He gets to know the secret springs that influence, and how to touch them with a delicacy that evokes no harsh responses. The fact that he comes to look upon men as instruments upon which he can play frees him from the most prolific cause of discords in life, that sense that there must come from every associate an agreeable reaction. He expects nothing in the way of reaction further than the effect he wishes to produce. He impresses himself upon the people consciously. He plays for certain responses. He never launches himself without knowing where he should land. If he misses his anticipated moorings he is philosophical, and remembers that he is at fault. He does not get sore. He does not demand that all follow him. He observes the direction of the current, and either floats along with it or seeks to turn it by gentle and skilfully applied methods.

The real advertising man does not impose himself upon life. He observes it. He puts himself deliberately

The Advertising Man

into the current. He does not believe that all men should be as he, nor as his ideal. He assays them as they are, or as they appear to be. He does not hope to reform the world, but to sway and influence a few. He studies people to discover what are their springs of action, what it is that moves them most surely. He likes nearly all kinds of people, because he looks beyond what they do to discover why they do it. He tries to balance motives and acts. He estimates human nature. He woos the philosophic spirit, because he knows that worry on account of failures makes other failures inevitable. He believes in goodness because it is power, and finally because it is goodness.

The real advertising man is not a paragon of virtue. He is what he is, because he has learned to regard men and their doings as resulting from certain laws and tendencies. He does not charge all persons with their acts. People to him are volatile impulses and motives. The individuals are behind all mani-festations, not to be held responsible for much that is rated as personal acts. He thinks in terms of humanity rather than in terms of humans. A man to him is an atom of humanity. He thinks in terms of masses of men, and relates individuals to the averages of the masses.

In the world of sociology and religion the different professors think in the terms of their particular call-ings. The preacher thinks in terms of religion, the psychologist in terms of the automatic mind, the moralist in terms of the Decalogue. The advertising man is all of these, and more. He sees religion as one of the elements of living, ethics as another, and the automatic actions of the mind as the machinery for the assimilation of all the motives and happenings of life. He realizes that all sciences and moralities and religions are elements in life, but that none of them *is* life. He must consider the man as he lives, because if he does otherwise he will not be able to get at the man and induce him to act.

So the real advertising man, who realizes his vocation, is bound to be an individual with qualities that are distinctive, that are different, that are sometimes remarkable and remarkably effective and enjoyable. He is bred to accomplish things; so in whatever relation of life he applies his energies he is apt to be doing things, rather than dreaming and talking about doing them. In this function the advertising man is a great asset to society. He is always a social being, and he is always working for some social object. He is an uneasy element wherever he is. Whatever measure of fame or degree of notoriety other able citizens attain, the advertising men in any community are always well known, and well liked.

There are many men in the advertising business who are not advertising men. They go through the motions during the day, and then subside into their natural state, whatever that may be. They are misplaced. Some accident made them shadows of advertising men, and, as shadows are as substantial as they are, they remain in the business, though not of it. They may be burglars or vestrymen, gardeners or hen-raisers, bookmen or machinists—they are not real

The Advertising Man

advertising men. They are admirable husbands and citizens, but they are not among those who look at life as those we are thinking about, and they are not esteemed as consequential in the business.

It is one of the present advantages of the advertising profession that there are not in it any professors, in the usual sense—men bred up for the work. The men who are now vital in advertising are vital because they are naturally fitted for it, and have not been molded and shaped for their niches. This condition will be changed. There are many movements on foot to train youth to become advertising men—to take the willing fellow and teach him how it is done. When these fledglings of the schools come into the business it will change. They will know how to plan a conventional campaign, how to construct the copy for the advertisement, and how to lay it out for the printer. What they will not know is how to get that keen and acrid flavor of life that the present advertiser has discovered enables him to be a real advertising man. There is much that can be taught to qualify a youth for the work of leading crowds up to the counters of trade, but that which is most vital is not to be taught in schools.

The real advertiser delights to lead men, as do the real preachers, the real lawyers, the great evangelists of religion, ethics and business. It is food and drink to him to note that he is able to move people, to get them acting as he suggests. To this end he studies them. It is not important that an advertising man should know how to write copy, or how to specify the display for the printer. There are many who are not advertising men who can do these things. Schools of advertising would need to take their students and observe them for a series of months, and then send 90 per cent of them to learn other vocations. The training of advertisers is subordinate to the selection of the subjects for the training.

XI

How the People Take It

Just how deeply the public is interested in advertising is a matter which, as Dundreary used to say, "No feller can find out." There is much speculation and assertion, but there is nobody who knows. Many people read the advertisements, but how many, compared with the number that read newspapers and magazines? How many people read street-car cards, billboards, the circulars strewn on the porches of our houses? Women read the advertising that appears in their evening papers, and some of that which appears in the magazines. They read more advertisements than do the men. Look along the aisles of the cars on the suburban trains any morning, and note the few men who seem to be paying attention to the advertisements; yet if there is a new safety razor to be put on sale that morning, and liberally advertised in the papers, nearly all the men on the train will know about it before they debark at their station. In the process of turning the sheets of the voluminous morning papers of the big cities most men absorb some degree of consciousness of some of the advertising. And when they wish for socks they think of the advertised brands, because the advertisements have crept into their minds and installed there the names of those socks.

A nervy young merchant wished to "splurge" on a sale of left-overs, but the senior frowned upon the suggestion. The young man carried his point, and spent some $2,500 in Sunday papers to announce the special sale for Monday morning, despite the protests of the elder, who thought the money was wasted. There was $9,000 sales before noon that Monday, showing that some people had read the advertising. This is typical of department store advertising. It is a variety of publicity that attracts instant attention, and is, so far as it is well done, sure to bring returns. Advertising is as necessary for the department store as stocks of goods. It covers the ground all the way from the artistic and skilful work for the Marshall Field and Wanamaker stores to the mere lists of goods and "cut" prices for the "emporiums" of New York's East Side.

The response of the public to advertising is one of the mysteries of the times. Why do the people rush to buy advertised goods in one instance and neglect the invitations of other advertisements? Why, when they do respond to advertising, do they so often leave their judgment and common sense at home? Why should it be possible for a cheap department store to sell many gross of a cheap scarfpin at twice the regular retail price, merely by announcing that its "value" was more than the price asked?

Consider how small a proportion of the readers of newspapers and periodicals pay any attention to the advertisements. Suppose a clothier advertises a sale of 1,000 overcoats in newspapers having a million readers. If he sells all the overcoats he thinks himself lucky, and he is lucky. His return is but one-

How the People Take It

tenth of one per cent of the potential readers of his advertisement. If one per cent of the readers of the papers had read the advertisement, and one per cent of those who read the advertisement had bought overcoats, the overcoats would all have been sold. Is this a good way to figure the pulling power of an advertisement? It might work with overcoats and fail with shoes. It is the commonest experience of beginners in advertising that they get absolutely no response. They dodge into advertising, venture a timid little try-out, get no response, and join the ranks of the also-tried. Probably the greatest proportion of advertising money that is wasted comes from these people who never ought to have tried advertising

It is not so many years since the general estimation of advertising was that it was a method of defrauding people. There are many who think that way now ; and they are justified by a too large proportion of the bulk of the advertising that appears in the so-called "mediums." It is not that this proportion of advertising is intended to defraud, but that it is based upon the old idea that to be effective advertising must deal in superlatives, and offer more than there is any hope of delivering. There is the open or disguised promise of more than the goods will justify, the allurement of the exceptional value. The advertisement that describes an article and fixes the price at what it is worth, and says so, is almost unknown. There is the bait, and the bait is often in the form of allegation of exceptional value.

Advertising

In the minds of intelligent buyers this margin of untruth is reckoned. They discount the allegations of advertisers. They assume that there is an element of exaggeration and untruth in advertising, expressed or implied, and they form their judgments and regulate their actions accordingly. This element of untruth in advertising is very subtle, and very hard to locate. In many of the advertisements of the better class of stores and manufacturers, there is no word used and no proposition presented that is not true. Yet their advertising is sometimes vitally misleading and untrue. There is in many advertisements an assumption of virtue that is unwarranted. The assumption, for example, that Robinson's is a superior store is always present in the advertising of that store; and in some ways the store is different from others. The assumption of super-excellence in all the policies of the store is assiduously driven into the consciousness of the readers of the advertisements. It is the chief aim of the advertising to create a mental atmosphere of superiority in the mind of the reader. The policy extends to the attitude of the salesmen and women in the store, who exert themselves to make the customers at home and at ease. The goods sold in this store are no better than the ordinary department store goods, nor less in price. The bait of this advertising is a variety of untruth, if we are going to be very strict in definitions. There is the implication that different and better treatment and goods are to be found at this store, and the implication is about all there is to it. There is a hope

How the People Take It

of preference built up by the advertising, but there is no preference.

The people who read the advertising in the papers, the magazines, the street cars, on the billboards, and who get the announcements and circulars sent in the mail, learn to make allowance; to know about the percentage of untruth employed by the different big advertisers, and discount their statements accordingly. But this modicum of falsehood in so many advertisements breeds in the minds of people an equalizing feeling of distrust of all advertising, and all advertising is to some extent automatically discredited.

People who have become sophisticated look with suspicion upon advertising. The suspicion may not find expression in words, or be consciously entertained. Yet down in the bottom of the minds of the readers there is a feeling that whatever the advertisement may say they would like to see the advertised article before buying it. Such a feeling of distrust does not limit our faith in the statements of friends, nor does it attach in anything like the same degree to the news we read in the newspapers, notwithstanding our firm conviction that the newspapers have a very poor regard for the truth. We feel that the selfish motive of the advertiser inevitably leads him to make statements intended to lead us astray as to the actual value and usefulness of the thing he advertises.

The advertisers are always trying to "paint the lily." Notwithstanding the fact that they have become converted to "truth in advertising" they continue to make this subtle variety of untruth the leading attractive quality of their advertising. Descriptive and qualifying adjectives have not the value in advertising given them in other reading matter. The superlative in advertising does not convince readers; it is as likely to implant distrust in their minds. There is one very big concern that has made several fortunes through advertising, that has never exaggerated and never told untruths. It has assumed that people have sense and know how to discriminate. Its advertising is accepted at its face value. There are a few others whose advertising is read in entire faith in its *bona fides*. The whole commercial world knows what real advertising truth has done for these concerns, yet the average advertiser still believes that there must be an element of untruth in his advertising or it will not "pull."

While advertising is not accepted at its face value by the masses of newspaper and periodical readers, it is read with keen interest by a proportion of them. The advertising of several big stores in different cities is one of the more interesting features of the newspapers so fortunate as to print it. One never thinks of neglecting it. There are in the metropolitan newspapers always two or three advertisements that are as interesting as anything in those sheets. There are men in the business of advertising writing whose work averages with any literary work in any of the high-class periodicals. They have acquired a style—a felicity of language, a capacity to say what

they wish to say, a power to put a few words into
a form that makes a great impression on the readers,
the art of making words express shades and color-
ings of meaning—which enables them to turn out
pastels in prose, poetry in description, arguments
in solution, lure, persuasion, and conviction, in such
guise that its purpose and leading is almost forgotten in the pure joy of reading English so subtly
molded to the motive of the composition. In none
of the literature of the day has the language been
so modified for the expression of the thought in
the mind of the writer as in advertising; and nowhere has the idea of shaping the language of an
idea to slip easily into the consciousness of the
reader been so perfected.

There are in the service of the large advertisers,
and of the advertising agencies, a new and significant
variety of litterateurs, men and women who are able
to so manipulate the English language as to make
the shade of James Howell turn green with envy.
They make a close study of the meanings of words,
and what words may be made to mean when placed in
the right juxtaposition. They become very skilful in
making a few words mean as much as a sermon, and
carry as positive a motive as a real estate deed or
an act of congress. They are able to phrase an announcement with a few words so that it will suggest
the character of a commodity so clearly, and create
in the mind of the reader so definite a desire, as to
powerfully suggest an order. They have to build up
in the mind of the reader a perfect image of the

Advertising

advertised article, or its distinctive quality, and at the same time to so work upon the motor of the mind as to get it to prompt the purchase.

This is a difficult thing. It seems to be impossible; but if writers of advertising are not able to do it they are not fit for their task. That it is done suggests one way in which advertising is modifying business and social life.

In the older method of contact of mind and mind, one mind emptied itself in the presence of the other without preparing the way into it, trusting that some part of the message would go home and perform its mission. The astute advertiser follows another method: He first discovers what is the disposition of his prospect, what are his habits of mind, what is the easy road into his mind, what it is necessary to do to get him thinking in the right way— in short, how the mind can be prepared for the message he wishes to lodge in it. The modern salesman is obliged to adopt the same methods. Between the salesman and the advertiser there is being introduced into the world a different method of persuasion, and its application is becoming more and more universal each year. Ultimately, this modification of the intercourse of people will have its effect upon all phases of life. Sometime the preacher will not dare to depend upon fervor, spirituality and eloquence, to influence his flock into the better way of life, but will have to study methods of getting his message into minds that have been fertilized and cultivated for its reception in the manner the advertisers now practice to soften the soil of the minds of the people for the reception of their pleas to buy.

Advertising methods, and the acute if shallow researches of the advertising men, have been instrumental in bringing the principles of psychology, so far as they teach methods for controlling minds and suggesting actions, into the affairs of everyday life. Whether or not they are to be thanked for this is not yet clear. They have imposed a condition upon our business life that is important, and likely to importantly modify methods and theories. Whether or not we are inclined to make a study of this more or less new idea of getting inside the minds of the people we deal with, by methods almost as definite and prosaic as those we employ in splitting a log for the living-room fire, the principles of psychology are now available to everybody, and those whose watchword is "hustle" are grasping them, with varying degrees of understanding, and applying them to their business methods with great enthusiasm and persistency.

We are in the midst of a somewhat misty and uncertain era of mind influence—in business, in social life, and in the realms of ethics, morals, and religion. It is the advertising man who has precipitated us into this era. What the outcome will be we do not know, except that we will never return to the former more simple, if less effective, methods of selling our goods and of converting our neighbors. There has been injected into the veins of the body politic a virus that will work some kind of permanent change; for the better we hope, but, for better or worse, a radical and drastic change.

Up to a recent time the public has received advertising very much in the manner of the forcible feeding of suffragettes in the English gaols. It has not asked for it, it has not wanted it, and in many of its phases has vigorously protested against it. No mercy has, however, been shown. The billboards are yet by almost every roadside, the hoardings are on almost every blank wall, the compounds for the "cure" of almost all the ills known to man are still heralded on the pages of many newspapers, the street cars are still decorated with the amazing declarations of specific, cosmetic, commodity, process, and suggestion, and the blank spaces along the city streets are blazoned with electric signs. Whether we will or not, we are advertised at from every vantage and angle, in every place, and on every occasion. The most persistent book agent is obliged to get consent before he can bore a person with the tale of his wares, but the advertiser does not ask whether or not you like it—he slams his story into your face.

There is a faint sentiment seeping into the minds of some shrewd advertisers and publishers that this may not be altogether wise. A more insinuating approach is being cultivated by some advertisers, and some publishers of advertising mediums are beginning to restrict the variety of advertising taken. This movement is as yet scarcely discernible, except as noted in the case of trade journals. It is in the nature of a reaction from the public, which is getting into the condition known as "clied," when pigs are in mind. The public has been getting too much advertising, and is crying for less. This cry will get more insistent as time goes on, and finally advertisers will become conscious of it, and will heed it—to their own profit.

Not too many things have been advertised, but some things have been advertised too much. In the happy advertising future there will be a great many more advertisers, and many less "double-spreads." This is one of the matters that the public, in its reception of modern advertising, is attending to, slowly but efficiently. In the end, any appeal must be made in the terms of the parties appealed to. If the public is to be depended upon to respond to advertising, advertising must ultimately be shaped to suit the tastes and temper of the public. At present many advertisers seem to consider the buying public in the light of a crowd of people who must pass through the turnstiles they have erected, and deposit coins for the privilege. Many publishers of advertising mediums (newspapers and other periodicals) appear to believe that they have collated their subscription lists for the benefit of the concerns that advertise in their pages, and therefore support them. They get together a company of people, secure entry into their homes, and say to the advertisers, "Here are so and so many people who have got some money you can get if you advertise with us."

People are beginning to become sensitive to these

methods of the advertisers. They know that they do
not have to buy the advertised things, but they do
not enjoy being constantly told how unwise or im-
provident they are if they do not. The constant
trickle of command to buy gets on the nerves of some
readers, and they begin to look upon the advertising
section with relative hostility. They hate to have
the advertisers get their feet in so that they cannot
close the doors of their minds to the insistence. As
they make this growing aversion to too much pressure manifest, the advertisers and publishers who
are wise will try to modify the great burden of advertising, in volume and character. How delightfully
refreshing it will be when publishers of great magazines and papers declare that they will accept only
advertisements of such goods as their readers require
to satisfy their needs, and as are consonant with
the character of their periodicals!

Wise advertisers are taking account of the grad-
ual education of the public in advertising methods,
and its slow formulation of its degree and methods
of acceptance of advertising. They realize that advertising cannot be administered to the public as an
alterative is administered to a person with disordered
insides. Not only must the advertisement be agreeable
to the palate as it is being taken, but its ultimate
effects upon the economy of the body politic must be
good. If advertising produces economic nausea, without salutary after effects, that advertising should not
be imposed upon the people. It is deleterious to the
advertiser and to the medium. Some investigation in

this direction is being made, but it is to be noted that the investigation by the great advertising-medium publishers and the big advertising agencies is along lines that tend to discover and uncover for the advertisers the ultimate dollar of the consumers. There is this feeling growing up in the public mind, directed against the big magazines and newspapers. Those mediums are bought for another purpose than to make them cash carriers, taking from their readers and delivering to the advertisers. This dawning sense of being "worked" a bit too hard by the periodicals and the advertisers will in due time have its effect upon advertising.

XII

The Need of Research

The advertising men who are students of the conditions that affect their profession are advocates of analysis as applied to problems they have to solve, but not excessively so as regards the business itself. The reason for this indifference with regard to the ordered fundamentals of advertising lie on the surface. They will suggest themselves to those who are familiar with the present condition of advertising, and with its history.

There is a certain amount of research work being prosecuted in the field of advertising. Several professors of psychology connected with the lesser colleges and universities have been making experiments and investigations along sectional lines, and in the larger institutions the subject is attracting some attention, chiefly outside the strict university work of the professors or instructors interested. In Columbia two or three of the professors have been doing useful, if sporadic and inconclusive, work, chiefly as leaders of classes formed among practical advertising men for the purpose of special study of certain phases of their work. Such, for example, was the interesting and valuable work of Professor Frank Alvah Parsons in his study with a class in "The Principles of Advertising Arrangement"; the work of Professors Strong and Hollingworth of Columbia with similar classes, and the more extensive work of Professor Walter Dill Scott of the Northwestern University,

The Need of Research

who has published two or three volumes. **Professor**
Münsterberg of Harvard has given the matter **of**
psychology of business some slight attention, **and**
Professor Edmund Burke Huey of the Western University of Pennsylvania has published a book upon
"The Psychology and Pedagogy of Reading," which
has a great though incidental value as a section of
that thorough treatment the matter deserves. There
are a number of interesting books that have been
written by laymen which are of some value, but which
do not contribute materially to what we may call a
comprehensive survey of advertising, as a business
partaking of psychology so largely as we suspect
it does. These books are more in the nature of personal experiences and impressions, and impress one
as being dogmatic without making it apparent that
their writers have warrant for dogmatism, and inconclusive because they do not in the beginning lay
down the principles according to which they have
worked. One of these books may be mentioned as a
departure from the usual method of treatment. Paul
T. Cherington, connected with the Harvard Gradu-
ate School of Business Administration, has compiled
a book that is of considerable interest, called "Advertising as a Business Force," which consists of a
series of excerpts from advertising periodicals joined
with explanatory comment, the whole forming something in the nature of a case book. It is of use to
practicing advertising men, as most of the citations
are from reports of successful experiments in advertising. Its value from the point of view of a scien-

[165]

tific interpretation of the fundamentals of advertising is not apparent, and it is probable that that was not a part of the author's intent.

It is not bits of experience that are needed to form a theory of advertising that will account for its present development and lay down principles for its future. Experience in advertising has been along lines not developed from methodical study, nor indeed through careful analysis of such records of experience as are available. The results of successful experience are faulty, because they usually omit to mention the preceding experimentation and the methods that led from non-success to success, and because it is often the impulse of the reporter to withhold such data as does not tend to prove his postulate.

Practically all the data available for estimating the efficiency of advertising is *ex parte* evidence. The data that would shed reliable light on this wonderfully interesting problem is held as private property, in the records of concerns that have been experimenting on their own account and for their own benefit. They are not willing to submit their data to investigators who are not backed by responsible institutions. There has as yet been no request for it on the part of representatives of universities, or of well-based organizations within the ranks of the advertising fraternity. It is time there was some well conceived and properly financed movement to ascertain the nature and capacities of advertising, and formulate the results in a terminology that will be understandable by the practitioner as well as by the student.

The Need of Research

The matter of research work in the advertising field has for a long time engaged the attention of some of the more earnest students in the profession. It comes to the fore occasionally, at the meetings of the larger organizations, but the interest in it has thus far been purely academic; there has been no definite effort to inaugurate the movement that is of all the activities of the organized profession the most important to its permanence and profitable operation.

But this delicate matter should not be left to the advertising man. In its prosecution he should have but the part of adviser. The work should be conducted by one of the universities, and under the guidance of a competent professor of psychology with the mental equipment and habits of Professor Münsterberg. It is a work eminently worthy of the greatest university in America. There is nothing at present attracting attention in the field of sociology that so nearly touches the lives of the people as does advertising. It is revolutionizing family economics. It is making of life a very different problem than that which faced our fathers. It is deflecting our morals, and causing us to look upon the great problems of life through glasses that are ground according to no authorized prescription. There is almost nothing that is purchased for personal or family consumption that is not offered through advertising, or that is not manufactured and marketed with the advertising necessities of the case entering in as a controlling consideration. Let serious men or women think for a moment of their own experiences. How much do they buy that is not suggested by advertising in sight, or suggestions that advertising has poured into their minds? What do they do that is not in some measure the act of assenting to advertising suggestion? Where do they go that they are not in some degree obeying the mandates of advertising?

What would be revealed to us if this overshadowing influence of advertising in our lives could be searched out, digested into facts and stated in terms we could understand? If we were to try and compute the cost of advertising, directly and indirectly, in our modern lives, what would we discover? It is not that advertising is directly charged up to the consumer that forms this margin of added cost of living. We are told that if our breakfast foods were not advertised they would cost us more, because advertising creates great businesses and therefore proportionately reduces the unit cost. Fallacious logic! If it were not for advertising we would not be using breakfast foods, or at least would be eating the hominy, crushed wheat, or rolled oats, of the time anterior to advertising. Now we must have a variety of foods for the breakfast table, and it is advertising that forces them into our larders. We are all using and wearing and eating many things that have been imposed upon our lives through advertising, and many of them have now become necessities.

If this one phase of advertising—its real relation to our economic lives—could be definitely ascertained and clearly stated on both sides of the question, it

The Need of Research

would be a revelation that would astonish us all, and shock some. There are two sides to the question, of course; and it is not to be denied that the advantages resulting from advertising might outweigh the disadvantages. Perhaps chemistry might convince us that the sanitary carton which encloses our foods is worth all it costs, but scientific research would establish the cost to us, as well as accurately ascertain the benefit. We do not take the trouble to think of these effects of advertising. We do not take pains to estimate the benefit it is to us. We do not know what it means to us; and we should know.

Taking a purely professional view of the matter, it is made evident that the processes of advertising are tremendously extravagant. It costs the advertiser far too much for the benefit it gives. When there is something like a 75 per cent waste in advertising costs, it seems that the time is near when advertisers must themselves take some measures to discover why there is such waste, and how it may be avoided.

The most important, as well as the most interesting, phase of advertising about which we know little, and should know much, is its effect upon individual and social character. How is this great stream of suggestion, pouring into the minds of the people all the time, to the exclusion of the influences that have been dominant in the formative forces from time immemorial, affecting humanity? Is it building character, enhancing strength, developing bodies, broadening thought, clarifying emotions, sweetening dispositions, developing charity and love? Is it en-

[169]

couraging selfishness and greed, exciting passion,
encouraging irreligion, increasing extravagance and
gluttony and lust? It is affecting us in almost every
relation and moment of life. How is it affecting us?
That is what we do not know. We ought to know,
in order to adjust our lives to the new force that is so
insistently interfering with them.

This is the most interesting problem in sight to
engage the attention of the sociological investigator.
It suggests opportunities that are quite unique. It
offers an open door to fame. The other great sociological questions have been at least stated, and some
progress toward their full exploitation has been
made. Even the question of feminism is on the way
to a stage at which it will be thought of in similar
mental terms by all of us, and the necessary postu-
lates and arguments are being marshalled for our effort at decision. We see the light in politics, and
we get glimmerings of the onward path to be trod
by religion. We are able to submit ourselves to different influences in these matters, and make some
kind of an argument in defense or explanation of
our course. But we cannot resist the influence of advertising in our lives, nor can we estimate or explain it. It is the great sociological mystery. What
does it do to us, how does it do it, and why? We are
not able to answer these questions.

It is possible to aver that we are not affected by
advertising, but we cannot even make the statement
without availing ourselves of some of the things advertising has imposed upon us. If we speak it, it is

The Need of Research

possible that our enunciation is made clear and crisp because we are wearing some dental device that has come to us through advertising. If the allegation is written, we use several advertised things—paper, pencil, fountain pen, a form of enclosing envelope, a peculiar printed or engraved heading, ink that would never have been known to us but for an advertisement, etc. There is not a thread of our clothing but is ours because of advertising methods. We rarely eat a mouthful of food that does not come to us, directly or indirectly, through advertising. The very Bible we read, and all other literature, is advertised. Practically everything we take or do to preserve our health is advertised.

It is not necessary to assume that this advertising dominance is good or evil. It has built up a great wall of custom over which we cannot go, and beyond which is a country of habit and custom that has grown strange to us—unknown to our children and a mere memory to us. It is in and of us. We are optimistic enough to believe it is for good, and will work out in a manner to help us on and up. But we don't know. We want to know. We have a right to know. We see much, and suspect much that we do not see. We see only results, and only glimpses of results. We have to guess, to imagine, to accept raw assertions, to do without knowledge, because, while there are investigators and agencies that lay bare to our gaze all other relations of life, all other social phenomena, all other religious and moral problems, there is as yet none to tell us about advertising.

[171]

Advertising

The great association of advertising men, 12,000 strong they tell us, has issued its creed in favor of truth in advertising. Why it has done so we are not told. By what process of reasoning these men have come to the conclusion that truth in advertising is desirable for the advertiser and him advertised to, we do not know, and they do not know. They are right, of course. It is better to tell the truth than to lie, even in business—even in the advertising business. But how much better is it? How much more effective is the truthful advertisement than that which skilfully and agreeably lies? It is not proved that it is any better, for the advertiser. There is a very large body of experienced evidence to prove that a plausible lie, agreeably stated, is a great advertising force. It is so great that many make use of it, and shudder at the remote possibility of having to abandon it. The men who in convention declare for the truth in advertising wink at the falsehoods, direct and implied, in their own advertising. Why are we told that truth is mighty in advertising, and will prevail? Is the statement itself true, in its essence? If it is, then we are to look for literal truth in all the advertising handled by members of the association that has adopted truth as its shibboleth. If they are not prepared to make literal truth the basis of their advertising, it follows, does it not? that in adopting the shibboleth they are merely perpetuating the false in advertising that it is supposed to be a protest against.

There is a great psychological principle working

The Need of Research

in this matter, but we do not know exactly what it is nor what it means. Some research agency should become interested in it. The natural and logical solution is that the advertising interests undertake a research work that shall be broad enough to standardize and regulate their practice and at the same time furnish the public this information about the effect of advertising upon the social body which it does not now have. There is a difficulty, however. Such an investigation would reveal the wastes in the advertising methods, and the elimination of the wastes would deprive many periodicals of their advertising, and probably operate to diminish the volume of advertising in all, or nearly all, mediums. Making advertising efficient would reduce its volume. It would take some advertisers out of the field, and reduce the amount done by many. It would also, if the teachings of the results of the investigation were heeded, bring many new advertisers into the field. It would so change methods as to disorganize, for a time, not only the publications that exist on advertising but the agencies, and the methods of many lines of business. All the forces of the business will resist real research work, and be more or less justified in doing so. Therefore it is to other agencies that we must look for research in the field of advertising.

XIII

Present-Day Mediums

The mediums for advertising—the avenues through which it reaches the people—are several and varied.

There are the newspapers, thought by their proprietors to be the only proper, profitable, and legitimate mediums; the weekly and monthly so-called literary periodicals, of general circulation, also thought by their proprietors to be the only proper, profitable, and legitimate mediums; the trade and class papers; the street cars; billboards; electric street signs; novelties, circulars, pamphlets and booklets, form letters, and the many other devices and methods for getting the plea of the advertiser into the minds of the people who form the purchasing masses.

Practically all these mediums exist because they are advertising mediums. The newspapers and periodicals have another excuse in pleading their cause with the people who buy them. The newspapers are the palladiums of our liberties, besides being newspapers. They publish the news of the day, the day before and the day after—such of it as they believe will be for our good and their glory. One of the newspaper publishers put the theory aptly when he said that if there was anything which he thought his readers should not read he did not allow it to be printed. Some of the newspapers do print "all the news that's fit to print," so far as their editors are able to judge. Whether or not they print all the news, they are very efficient advertising mediums, as anybody can learn by reading their advertisements of themselves. It is doubtful if there is a considerable class of people that wants all the news, and it is more than doubtful if there is, ever was or ever will be, editors who know absolutely what is news. Nobody else knows, and it is not reasonable to suppose that an editor knows more than his readers! That which is news to one man does not in the least interest another. That is news to a person which confirms him in his ideas of what is news, or helps him demonstrate his theories of life and the universe. It is also news if one's political party wins an election. It is news to me if a friend of my boyhood who has stayed in the old town paints his barnyard fence; but no news to my wife, because she spent her youth in another town. That is news which interests readers, and not all of any newspaper's readers can be interested in the same things or in the same ways. No newspaper can possibly print all the news, fit or unfit. That newspaper whose editors can guess what will interest the greatest number of people is the best selling newspaper; but the best advertising medium is that newspaper which gets closest to its readers, and inspires them with the greatest confidence in what it prints.

The advertisement is like the chameleon—it changes its character with the medium in which it is printed. The character of the newspaper fixes the character of the advertisements printed on its pages, and vitally influences the returns flowing from them. A clean, honest newspaper yields more to its advertisers than does a paper that is not trusted or is not scrupulously clean. An advertising medium is valuable as such in a very direct ratio to its character and circulation. The public, besides being credulous and willing to swallow almost every kind of advertising bait, is sensitive and finicky. Because it is willing to buy a newspaper on a street corner is no warranty that it will buy the wares advertised in that paper, or that it will give credence to that which is printed in it. It is the habit of men to like the vernacular of the gutter, but it is not their habit to turn to the paper of the streets for advice and guidance in making purchases for the home.

Newspapers are, within their limited field, undoubtedly the best advertising mediums. The retail merchant, the grocer, the marketman, the seller of any goods whose distribution area is coextensive with the field covered by the newspaper, would be unwise to take up advertising with any periodical medium except the newspapers. The manufacturer or dealer who wishes to appeal to the whole country or to any of its grand divisions would not be able profitably to use the newspapers. There has been much warm discussion of this point, as between the magazines and the newspapers. The magazines agree that they cannot successfully advertise an article intended for the consumption of a small section; while the newspapers believe that they are good advertising mediums for anything that is to be advertised. Nationally distributed products might, as a proposition of pure theory, be advertised in the newspapers. But inasmuch as so many papers would have to be used, and as the gross cost would be so immensely big, it is evident that for national advertising the newspapers cannot now be considered by advertisers who figure probabilities. If there comes a day when the newspaper proprietors are willing to work together and adjust their rates so that relatively as much territory may be covered by using groups of newspapers, or by using selected lists, as can be covered with the same money through the use of magazines and weekly papers, it will be possible for the newspapers to claim that they can furnish national publicity upon a usable basis.

On the other hand, there are very few of the weeklies or monthlies that can by themselves furnish national publicity. To get a thorough distribution of advertising a very careful selection of mediums has to be made. Some magazines are strong in one section and some in other sections. There is a profitable field into which none of the well known magazines effectively enter, which must be covered through what are called "mail-order" journals, or by the extensively circulated farm and class journals. The high-class magazines are read by one stratum of buyers, the weeklies by another, the cheap magazines by another, the mail-order papers by another; and the newspapers are read by all, but in isolated groups, so that their circulation is limited territorially while the magazine circulation is limited temperamentally.

Advertising

The newspapers of America are passing through a phase of development that is of peculiar interest. They have not yet become fixed as one of the social features of this country. They are in a condition of flux, as they have been since the elder James Gordon Bennett made up his mind to print the news in the New York *Herald*. At that time they had a period of big development as newspapers. Then they developed as mechanical propositions. Now they are developing as properties. Perhaps they will have another cycle of development as newspapers. Just now their growth as advertising mediums is their most significant feature, and it, coming on the heels of a very wonderful evolution of the machinery for producing them, is having a strong tendency to turn them in all departments into machines.

The element of strong personal leadership and manipulation, represented by such men as Greeley, the elder Bowles, the elder Bennett, Bryant, Childs, Raymond, McClure, Dana, and many others of that type, has been superseded by the astute business manager. The actual editors are little known in connection with big newspapers, though the breed is not yet extinct. The proprietor often takes the title of editor, while doing none of the editorial work. In most of the large papers the policy is decided by the business office; not always unwisely or devoid of ideals, but finally and inevitably. Nearly all newspapers are controlled by some well-defined policy, formulated by the owners and rigidly enforced. Even those papers that seem to be conducted on broad lines are always concerned for the income, and are what they are because their owners are big enough to understand that the greatest profit and influence must come through furthering the greatest good of the people who buy the paper.

The mechanics of editing the newspapers of today are behind those of one or two generations ago. The process of making newspapers has been reversed. Formerly they were made up of material that came to them in the form of news and reflective observation. They were, in a real sense, reflectors of the life of their times. Now they are reflectors of the policies of their owners. Their treatment of the news of the day is so different, one from another, that while they use the same basic material they each present a picture of the passing day that is distinctive. The big newspaper has its well-defined policy, its definite conception, as to what the news of the day shall be made to mean to its readers, and processes of editing are predicated upon that formulated conception. In one paper a certain event will be so "featured" as to appear the most significant thing for the readers' attention. In another paper, the same dispatch, received in identical length and expressed in identical language, may be relegated to an obscure position, cut down to an item, and honored with but a single-line heading. One paper "plays it up" in the news columns, and makes it the text for the leading editorial, and the other minimizes it.

A man connected with the editorial staff of one of the big aggregations of newspapers said: "We do not get instructions. I never had a word of advice or instruction from the Big Boss; but I know exactly what he wants. If I did not, and he thought that I did not, I would not be here. If I did not work along the lines of what I know to be his policy, I would not stay here."

The majority of the larger newspapers are operated in this smooth and brotherly fashion. Every morning or evening they appear, free and untrammeled, with all the news their conductors see fit to print. They are good newspapers, in our modern sense. They are not like the papers of the old days. In some ways they are better.

The use of the news of the day to make a newspaper, rather than the publishing of a newspaper for the purpose of disseminating the news, is the root of the evil of the newspapers. It is a real evil, greater than can be estimated through simply considering that each newspaper has its characteristic method of handling the news. It is one thing to handle the news, and quite another thing to manipulate the news. It is that the news is manipulated that forms the reproach of many of the papers. And not only that the news is manipulated, but that the tendencies and lessons of the news are not left to shape themselves in the minds of the readers. The newspapers insist upon their own interpretation, not only in editorial interpretation, but through all the delicate and subtle methods that have become so refined in newspaper offices. There is much matter published that has an entirely different psychological influence than that which would have resulted if it had not been molded, excised, tempered, edited, rewritten, reversed, or in some way made to convey an impression foreign to its obvious and natural meaning.

The great majority of newspapers are seldom tempted to ignore their convictions, because they are potent only in small communities. There are also many publishers who think of nothing but the pleasure and benefit of their readers. In this class are the thousands of country weeklies and small dailies. These papers are credited with great cumulative influence, and they are entitled to such credit. The great estimation of the influence of the local papers is, however, overdrawn. The weeklies have undergone a change, as have the dailies. They are not, as a class, as vital as of yore. The daily idea has crowded most of the large and influential weeklies out of existence. Where there were vital weeklies there are now small and not very vital dailies; and where these dailies have been started the weeklies have died.

The magazines are passing through parlous times. There are too many of them. The struggle for existence is too tense. They are too dependent upon advertising. Only a few of them can afford to sell at the price asked. The advertisers have to donate the difference. The advertisers have to pay for their sections of the magazines, pay a profit upon their proportion of production expense, make up the deficit the subscribers create, and pay all the profit on the section the readers should pay for. This makes the popular magazines advertising mediums first and vehicles of literature second. The magazines are conducted either from the counting-rooms or in complete sympathy with the wishes and necessities of the counting-rooms. The editors of the good magazines are able and honest. They have free rein; but they know what must be done. Nearly every magazine is edited to attract more readers. The literary motive is invoked to justify their work, not to control and suggest it. Every editor studies with nervous apprehension the whims and predilections of the people his owners wish to enroll as readers. He racks his brain to think of something that will be novel and different for his pages.

It is this quality that makes of the magazines the effective advertising mediums they are. They are so much closer to the people than they used to be, even if they are not as consistently literary. They have got so close to their readers that they now have a quality that periodicals never before had—the quality of being a vital part of life. They were, long ago, attributes of life. They were resorted to by their readers for a mild form of pleasure, for literature, for the diversion found in the mild and proper stories of those other days. Now the readers of magazines seek in them some element of their actual lives. They weep and swear over them, and resolve to fight for this or that reform. It is true that they still sigh with the ardent swain who is pursuing his sweetheart, and are exalted with the poet who aspires or rants.

Present-Day Mediums

But the swain in pursuit of his Dulcianea is also ex-
emplifying some great principle of eugenics, and the
poet is slamming some big social evil or abuse;
and so the reader, whether he will or not, is drawn
into the vortex of life, and must be stormed and
racked in its swirling depths.

Readers of periodicals are over-advertised. With
anywhere from 100 to 300 pages of advertising in a
popular magazine, it is unreasonable to suppose that
any announcement gets the attention it may intrinsi-
cally be worthy of. This is a matter that would not
interest publishers, as they must have a large volume
of advertising or go out of business. It does not
greatly interest advertisers, because they plan for
the consumer to pay for the advertising, and they
hunger for more and more business. It is a question that interests the long-suffering readers of
magazines and the students of advertising and sociology. Perhaps there will some time come upon the
stage a class of periodicals that will not print more
advertising pages than readers can comfortably examine, and will not allow on those pages advertisements in which readers may not be profitably interested. This kind of magazine, with a subscription
rate that will yield a profit on the reading section,
is an ideal that is not substantially in evidence,
though it is beginning to obtrude into the minds of
the more thoughtful.

One of the practices of periodicals, with reference
to their attitude toward advertising, that causes them
a great deal of trouble and that goes far toward fix-

ing their standing as advertising mediums in the
public mind, is their peculiar policy with reference
to charges for advertising space. In the good old
times, when advertising revenue was looked upon as a
gift from the gods, and when advertising was itself
looked upon as a species of not over polite graft
(which, *entre nous*, most of it undoubtedly was), the
tariff charges was based upon the publisher's idea
of what the traffic would bear. One line of business
was able to pay more than another, or was inclined
to submit to a larger rate. So there was a rate for
dry goods, a rate for banks, a rate for insurance
companies, a rate for legal notices, a rate for political notices, a rate for schools, etc. All these different lines of business bought exactly the same thing—
the privilege of speaking to the readers of the paper
or magazine or trade paper. They had the same kind
of space, it cost the same to print their announcements, and they had the same chance for getting returns. But they paid different rates. There was nothing to excuse this fashion then, and there is nothing
to excuse it now. It persists, especially in the newspapers. Many of the magazines—most of them, in
fact—have a "flat" rate, so called because they
charge a price for a page, and corresponding mul-
tiples of that page price for portions of a page;
with additional percentages for the "preferred" posi-
tions, such as the cover pages and the pages facing
reading pages, etc. They give cash discounts, and
some of them give discounts for quantity, for continuous publication, or on contracts calling for a

specific number of pages to be used within a certain specified time, such as six or twelve pages during a calendar year. Nearly all of the newspapers have a medley of rates. They charge one price for dry-goods stores, another for real estate. They have a dry-goods rate (in New York) for Harlem, different ones for Brooklyn, Jersey City, Manhattan, etc., and they have different rates for bank statements and other financial advertising, and another for publishers. To understand and remember the rates of a city newspaper is in the nature of a liberal education, and requires great capacity and quick responsive action on the part of one's subconscious mind, wherein we are told is stored everything we ever learned.

The magazines and weeklies are to be credited with leading in improvement in physical appearance. The newspapers have lagged, and are now not as attractively printed as were those of two generations ago. They have sacrificed everything to speed, even a desire to improve. On the other hand, the magazines are very handsomely printed. Some of them go far astray in search of spectacular effects, but even those are well printed so far as the execution is concerned. The magazine that is, all things considered, the best printed of all has a glaring defect in that it persists in the use of a type face not suitable for finished paper. All the magazines use a similar type face, but not all are in other respects so perfectly printed. The only magazine that uses type perfectly fitting for finished paper with illustrations, does not use finished paper or illustrations!

Advertising

If a group of the large magazines would correlate the elements of their physical being, with the discriminating taste and full knowledge they always display in the selection and preparation of their literary and artistic contents, they would be so nearly perfect as to make criticism impossible. Their elements are each well executed. Their composition is well enough executed, their presswork is excellent, their paper is as good as need be; but these elements are not coördinated, in an artistic sense. An artist would not permit in his composition a discord equal to the lack of harmony between type and paper seen in nearly all the magazines, nor would he tolerate anachronisms such as exist in the arrangement of their typography.

There is a class of advertising mediums that offers a very good illustration of this idea—the trade papers. This class of periodicals is the best existing example of advertising mediums that approach to a sane and commercial ideal. In the first place, the better trade papers serve their readers better than any other class of periodicals, not excluding the newspapers. They restrict their circulation to such people as are directly interested in the trade they serve. They do not encourage subscriptions from men who are not actively in the business they represent; and they know who their subscribers are. Some of the more progressive among them make their subscription lists a very accurate "who's who" in their trade. They are able to show just what is the position, the income, the history (in his trade), the capacity, the influence, etc., of every man who takes their papers. They make a very close and expert study of these lists. They do not encourage people to buy their papers who are not, in some vital manner, interested in them and the trades they represent, and who are not likely to be of value to the advertisers in those papers. They do not, of course, wish or assume to bar out men who do not buy the goods advertised, but they desire that their readers shall at least be of such vital interest to the advertisers as to keep in touch with the best progress made in their special fields, realizing that the intelligent man who operates machinery has, in the long run, some influence on its character and type, and will always be something of a factor in its purchase. To these strictly selected lists of readers the publishers of the good trade papers present only such advertising as they believe will interest and benefit them. While their readers are steady and heavy purchasers of general merchandise, and of all the things that are advertised in general periodicals, none of them will publish advertisements of patent medicines, proprietary articles, clothing, articles for personal use, etc.

That these papers confine their advertising strictly to things that are connected with the business they represent is an evidence of the shrewdness and breadth of view of their publishers. This policy makes of the advertising an integral part of the initial interest of the paper to its readers. They know that there is nothing in the pages of their

trade paper, reading matter or advertisements,
which is not of interest and value to them. Accordingly, the advertising in high-class trade journals
is effective beyond the percentage of efficiency shown
by the general periodicals.

As a whole, the trade-paper section of the
great periodical family is giving a most valuable
and significant demonstration of what the ideal advertising medium should be. Its principles are attracting attention outside its borders. It is doing much
more than simply to standardize advertising practice. It is standardizing periodical sizes and shapes;
and especially is it standardizing that extremely il-
lusive and flexible element of publishing—circulation statements. It is not only showing exactly what
the circulations of the papers are, in all of their
important elements, but it is formulating, adopting,
and imposing, standards for stating and valuing circulations which will have to be adopted by all periodicals hoping for large and permanent advertising
patronage.

The trade papers are also blazing the way to another radical reform in periodical publishing: A
small group of the more efficiently managed of them
has begun to study the field to discover what sort
are the people they must cater to, and just what
sort of trade literature they require. They desire to
produce such goods as will readily sell in their field.
This idea, that the magazine should be made for those
who are expected to buy it, is beginning to make its
way into the policy of the publishers of magazines

of general interest and circulation. A magazine intended for women, for example, commissions an expert in sociology to make a survey of a section in which there are 10,000 potential readers for his magazine, and digest his findings into a report that shall be a guide for his editors.

XIV

Mediums of the Future

A careful study of advertising as it is developing,
together with a corresponding study of advertising
mediums and their recent history, leads to a presump-
tive conclusion that the future development of advertising may proceed along lines that are not yet generally recognized.

It is agreed that advertising must be made more
efficient, and that in some manner the waste of nearly
75 per cent of the money expended must be reduced
to a reasonable percentage. Such waste is an economic condition repugnant to the modern conception of
business. If it cannot be substantially reduced, it
will be impossible to maintain that advertising is an
economical business element. The items of its constitution and practice that are opposed to economic
principles are apparent. Their cure is not as apparent. It offers to the business economist a problem
of special interest, full of baffling elements. It has
grown to its present great proportions through natural processes. Some advertisers have reaped great rewards, and that has established a vogue that has
drawn the great army of unsuccessful advertisers
into the business.

Progress is being made toward the solution of
some of the problems presenting themselves to advertisers, but it is not to the best advantage of investigation that they are in the hands of the parties
most in interest. While advertisers, through coöper-

Mediums of the Future

ative associations, are making valuable studies of phases of the question, they are for the most part accepting the question of mediums as it exists, only demanding that the mediums shall show their hands to the advertisers. They do not assume, and probably will not assume, to go to the bottom of the medium question in order to determine and enforce fundamental conditions. What those fundamentals are, or will be discovered to be, cannot now be fully stated. Some of them come automatically to the surface in consequence of the general agitation in all lines of investigation.

Newspapers appeal less acutely to classes of readers than any other advertising medium in the periodical field. Billboards, and all the so-called "direct" mediums, make their appeal to all who travel the highways, railroads, street cars, and streets. They are fairly to be considered for any use that involves the attention of any and all classes. The newspapers have broad zones of interest within definite borders running through the regions within which they are able to circulate. All newspaper readers buy something; a large proportion of the readers of all papers buy, or may buy, all things. Some newspapers are not good advertising mediums for books, and some are not effective for "chains" of groceries. Some are good for jewelers, and some pay this or that branch of trade better than other branches. This distinction is not the same in two cities. It must be determined with respect to each group of newspapers. It is not inherent in newspapers as newspapers. The cleavage

Advertising

is different as related to weeklies and monthlies of general, or geographical, circulation. Those magazines, weekly or monthly, which are sent all over the country are more strictly class publications, so far as their advertising influence is concerned, than are the newspapers, though as to general character of content they may not be so strikingly differentiated. Two weeklies, the *Outlook* and the *Independent*, to cite concrete examples, may be very similar in general purpose, in broad treatment of the affairs of the day, and as to literary ability and journalistic practices. Yet they have such distinct individualities, and their readers are so different in character and circumstances, as to make of them two very distinct advertising propositions. There are differences between all other periodicals which may seem to the superficial observer as belonging to identical classes, and this difference is often so subtle and obscure as to tax the keenest faculties of the most astute advertisers to detect it and govern their contracts accordingly.

In their advertising practice the periodicals do not sufficiently recognize these differences. They do not try to select their advertising patronage to correspond with the particular character of their circulation. There probably is not one magazine published but would claim that it is a good medium for Tiffany's advertising. That there is a magazine or weekly published that would reject a Tiffany contract is unthinkable. Yet there are many that should do so, as readily and inexorably as they reject the offers of the worst among the "cures" and fakes. It is as uneconomic, and as immoral, for the manager of a magazine whose readers are not in the Tiffany class to accept a Tiffany advertisement as for him to accept an advertisement for a cancer cure. It seems obvious that to promote the efficiency of advertising sufficiently to bring it into the class of economic business practice the periodicals must limit their acceptances to such business as they may have ascertained appeals profitably to their readers. That this is a hard condition to suggest does not take from its logical reasonableness. Advertisers are themselves working toward something like it. It is the business of the periodicals to specify and exhibit that which they have for sale.

This particular problem in applied advertising is not one that belongs exclusively to the magazines. It is a fundamental principle in advertising that belongs to the business generally, and its application is equally the business of all mediums and all advertisers. It is very well understood and very rigidly applied by the trade papers. Other publishers should study the methods and forms of these publishers, and apply them in their own business. When a big magazine, like the *Century*, for example, is able to give an advertiser as much information about its subscribers as the publisher of *Power*, for instance, is able to give, there is a reason for throwing the responsibility upon the advertiser. In the case of the literary magazines there is the uncertain element of the news stand sales. These would have to be taken on faith, but the analysis of the direct subscribers would cover the news stand buyers with approximate accuracy; though if the transient buyers were in a large majority there would be an element of vagueness which it would be somewhat difficult to deal with. But even this could be handled in a manner that would show quite closely the character of the readers of any periodical.

Such restriction of the volume of advertising as this would entail, would put many of the magazines in a very uncomfortable financial condition. They could scarcely endure the reduction, unless there were compensating circumstances. What these compensations might be is one of the problems of the situation. On the surface, it seems that the adoption of such a policy would result in the disappearance of many periodicals and the limiting of the business of those that remained. There is an alternative, of course. They might limit the expense of production, and especially of promotion. It is no secret that many of the popular periodicals now pay a very large percentage of their receipts for promotion, in their circulation and advertising departments. Readers come high. They are bought with prizes, cut rates, and combination subscriptions; and when their year expires they must again be bought in some similar way. Some periodicals get no more than 30 per cent renewals, upon any terms; while others get as high as 60 to 75 per cent of voluntary renewals. Periodicals that get the low percentage of renewals find their circulations a heavy burden upon their advertising income. Those that get the high percentage of voluntary renewals, at the published rates, may be able to figure that their circulations are not an expense to their advertisers. The trade papers get much higher percentages of renewals than literary periodicals, sometimes going above 90 per cent; and they usually get the full amount of their subscription prices, rarely allowing commissions to agencies or making combination rates.

The intelligent and economic selection of advertising for each periodical, based upon its ability to produce revenue for the advertisers, is a matter of much difficulty. It is not an academic proposition. It will be brought sharply to the attention of publishers by the advertisers. They are now thinking hard along these lines, and some of them are putting the principles suggested into practice. Such selection, if rigidly enforced, would justify a substantial increase of advertising rates, and thus the magazines might hope to recoup themselves for losses of advertising not suitable for them to publish.

Looked upon as a matter that, from its nature, should submit readily to scientific analysis, the whole question of advertising mediums is in an unsatisfactory and chaotic condition. Nothing is known about it except that which comes from the publishers and the experience of the advertisers. The authority of both these sources has not been determined. The statements made by the publishers are *ex parte*, and usually deal only with numbers. A few publishers make dissected statements, showing who their subscribers are, so far as occupation is concerned, and how they are distributed. The advertisers demand that they know the exact number of subscribers to the publication they propose to patronize, and the conditions under which the subscriptions were secured. They judge the character of the readers by the character of the periodical.

When all is said, advertising is human nature. If the advertiser knows human nature he does not need to study psychology, because that absolute science is merely a formulation of what students have discovered about human nature. The most expert psychologist in the world is he who is able to move his fellows in the direction he wishes them to go, through speech, example, or the written word. Psychology does not give the advertiser a knowledge of human nature. It, at the best, shows us how to apply our knowledge of human nature to get people to do what we wish them to do. The attempt to apply psychology, or any formulæ, to the work of advertisement construction, without a sympathetic knowledge of human nature back of it, usually lands the performer where the versifier who wrote these lines (J. F. T., in *Profitable Advertising*, August, 1908) found himself:

Mediums of the Future

I can write ads philosophical,
And deeply psychological,
But never tautological,
   To fill a given space.
I have a natural proclivity
For appeals to subjectivity,
Always read with keen avidity
   By all the human race.

With language iridescent
My ads seem incandescent,
Filled with sparkling, effervescent
   Thoughts galore.
And to frame up illustration
Is a pleasant relaxation,
Just esthetic recreation,
   Nothing more.

I believe, myself, implicitly
That I can get publicity
With ads of that simplicity
   For which the public yearns;
But though having each essential
That should make them influential
They don't seem so damn potential—
   For they never bring returns.

This sort of thing, which is very common in advertising, confounds those who believe there is a science of advertising being wrought out of experience and study, but who do not look deeply enough into the questions that science suggests to perceive that science is merely the arrangement of facts, with which it has nothing to do except to arrange. In advertising the most astute scientists are those who know how to read human nature; and this idea has also been expressed with much cleverness by another

Advertising

versifier (W. Livingstone Larned, in *Profitable Advertising*, March, 1909):

We took the little ad he ran
　And picked it all apart, I guess
We proved him up a foolish man
　And left the copy part a mess.
We told him his design was "punk."
　That artist should have pushed a plow.
But all he said when we were through
Was one-fourth wrong and three-fourths true:
　　"It's pulling, anyhow!"

We gave our space to solid chat
　And told how copy should be "writ."
We rapped his "selling plan" at that
　And didn't like the selling plan a bit.
We found a fault with "balance" and
　We knocked his picture of the plow.
But, at his flat-top desk he grinned
And said with reference to "wind,"
　　"It's selling, anyhow."

And so, ye wise ones with your ways,
　It might chance that the seer is wrong;
Full many ads run many days
　And somehow manage it along.
Dope out our "system" as we will,
　And to our brainy plans make bow.
What answer is there to the word,
The which the most of us have heard,
　　"It's paying, anyhow?"

XV

The Agents

The advertising agents form an element in advertising that has not been justly estimated. They have for some twenty years had great influence. They came into being as a purely speculative move, not particularly concerned with advertising except in a brokerage sense. They bought space in newspapers at wholesale rates and sold it at retail, not interesting themselves further. They did not prepare the copy for the advertising they handled, nor did they make advertising plans. They have progressed to their present estate through several phases of development. They are now a very important element in advertising; a very useful and necessary element, in their best estate.

The modern advertising agency is a many-sided organization. It solicits business, and handles it. That is, it gets the orders from the advertisers, writes and sets the advertisements, makes the illustrations if any are used, selects the lists of mediums (in connection with the advertisers or their representatives), issues the orders to the mediums, checks up the insertions, pays the publishers, and has charge of the details incidental to the business.

For this service the most modern and progressive agencies are paid by the advertiser, generally a certain percentage on the gross expenditure—from 10 to 25 per cent, according to the ability and reputation of the agent. This method of paying the agent is not universal. Some get salaries, as though they were of the executive staff of the business they advertise, and in these cases the advertising agent is frequently consulted with regard to sales plans, office management, efficiency measures, manufacturing, and especially selling. It is common to find the advertising agent, or manager, in close relations with the sales manager, and sometimes his virtual superior. Probably a majority of agents still continue to draw their commission from publishers, the usual rate being 13 per cent on the gross amount paid to the newspaper or magazine.

From being merely a broker in advertising space the modern advertising agent has come to be a producer of advertising business for the periodicals. He no longer acts as the agent for the periodicals. He is a creator of advertising business, and acts for the advertiser. He studies the problems of his clients, and recommends and executes advertising plans which his experience and knowledge persuade him are likely to be efficient. It is often the case that an agent will advise an advertiser that he should not use publications, and puts his business on billboards, in street cars, or makes use of circulars, letters, booklets, or catalogues; or even is content with the use of some attractive novelty, judiciously bestowed upon people whose trade is desired or who are in position to influence the trade of their friends. Good agents often advise would-be clients against advertising in any form, and instead suggest changes in methods of manufacture or selling that, in their particular cases, are equivalent to more direct methods of publicity in their effect on the business.

The advertising agent of the best type has a beneficent influence upon the periodicals he uses. He is able to give the publishers and editors the benefit of his close relations with the advertisers. He usually knows how the periodicals stand in the estimation of the public much better than any one connected with the periodicals can know, and his advice is often worth a great deal to them. It is the particular business of the advertising agent to study the effect of advertising upon the people who read it, or may read it. He, if he is progressive and intelligent, knows what is likely to be effective for a certain line of goods better than any other person who comes in contact with the advertising problem, and his advice should be the best available, for the advertiser and for the publisher.

As the agent holds the purse-strings for so many publishers it is reasonable to assume that his influence with them is considerable, but such is not always the case. Since the big advertising mediums have become so very big some of them are inclined to consider the agents in the light of an unnecessary evil, and they have begun to draw the lines of his sphere so rigidly as to make his work difficult and his profits precarious. The big publishers have gone into the agent's field and perfected plans and machinery for the purpose of creating new business and handling old business, relegating the agent to the plane upon which he began business—a filler of advertising

THE FIRST DUTY OF AN ADVERTISEMENT

CONSIDER the readers of a newspaper or a magazine: They are not looking for anything in particular. They are not wondering what you will say next. They have neither you nor your goods in mind at all They are not conscious of your existence.

The space you buy merely gives you an opportunity to arrest their attention as they casually turn the pages. The rest is up to you, but the rest must be right. Successful advertising is a peculiar mixture of practical merchandizing principles and business imagination. But success is always a question of degree, and the degree must depend upon a just appreciation of this mixture.

Gasoline, in its liquid form, is potential power, but it will not run a motor car. It must be exploded. Beware lest the concentration on merchandizing principles lets you forget the first duty of an ad, which is to arrest attention. If it fail, and that leaf be carelessly turned—all your thought, care, research, trade work—everything that has been so carefully expressed in the text—is lost. And the appropriation is lost. The reader passes on.

That is why we pay great attention to art, typography, display and atmosphere. It is primary and fundamental.

CALKINS & HOLDEN

250 Fifth Avenue New York

space, and acting for small advertisers who cannot afford to instal systems of checking and payment.

There is at present in the advertising field an uneasy and illogical movement of advertisers to and from the agents. Large advertisers are abolishing their independent advertising departments and turning their business into the agencies, relying upon their supposed expert knowledge, and merging their details into the organizations the agents must in any case maintain. This is the principle ostensibly underlying the trusts—coördination of selling interests and reduction of management expenses.

The handling of advertising does not lend itself to close coördination with the regular executive and administrative work of large concerns. It is work for specialists, even down to the routine of filing and correspondence. If concerns handle their own advertising, through an advertising manager, they must instal a separate and distinct department manned with people who cannot be of much use in other departments. The overhead of an advertising department is likely to be large, and not subject to reduction.

The psychology of the situation is also with the outside agent, who has an organization and who may be doing a far greater business than the concern whose advertising he proposes to handle. He has all the ear-marks of success, and the advertiser contrasts him with the man who is his advertising manager, and whose wife and babies, hopes and fears, good and bad qualities, he knows. And he knows the failures

of his personal advertising manager, just how much
that young man knows about advertising and just
how much he guesses about it. The outside agent is
an accomplished salesman of his own product. He
does not disclose his failures, and from his appearance and talk the advertiser infers that there are
none to disclose. He is a positive man, and gives
the advertiser to understand that nothing will be
allowed to trouble him, nothing be left for him to
decide, nothing given to the rapacious mediums that
can be kept from them, etc. So the capable man who
has devoted himself to a careful study of the advertiser's individual business is dismissed, and the business turned over to the agent, to be handled as one
cog in the machine.

In many instances, perhaps a majority of the
large advertisers, there is an advertising manager
maintained while the routine part of the work is
handled by an agency, obviating a special department in the business office, but retaining the invalu-
able services of the man who makes an intimate and
sustained study of the business. The mediums are
selected by the advertising manager, sometimes in
consultation with the agent, and the agent sends
out the orders, checks the insertions and pays the
bills.

There are many variations on these different methods. In many cases the agents do everything except
fix the amount of the annual appropriation; in some
cases they even have a very large influence upon this
fundamental function. They study the business, in

the light of advertising principles they may have
formulated from their practice, make the general advertising plans, select the mediums, write the copy,
and do all of the work. The principals are not annoyed with any of the details; they do not have to
struggle with the new science of selling, which they
do not understand, and do not wish to understand.
They pay the bills, in the form of monthly checks
to their agent, and they enjoy the resulting increase
of business. They look upon advertising as an expense, made necessary by the new-fangled ideas
about business, but not nevertheless to be wholly
approved.

The modern advertising agent is a very able and
long-headed business man, sometimes touched with
the fire of an exalted altruism that has been working its way into advertising, but not by that in-
capacitated from making the best bargain for himself the business warrants. He understands human
nature, both of buyers and sellers, of the advertiser
no less than of the advertisee. He knows more about
the publishing business than the executive secretaries
of the publishers' associations. He knows the strong
and the weak points of the advertisers, and of their
goods. He knows the public, and how to sway it
to attention for the advertisements he makes and
places. He is usually a man of strict probity, and
always renders unto Caesar the things that are
Caesar's—and keeps the things that he believes are
the agent's. He is a diplomat among men, knowing
just where to put a little pressure, and how to apply

a bit of blarney. He must sell his goods to men who are past masters in the art of selling; and he must therefore be a 100 per cent salesman. His personality is like a human magnet—suggestions come to him from all people and under all circumstances. He is a man with broad and deep vision. He has imagination. The chance remark at the lunch table expands and works out in his mind until upon its big screen there is a vivid and detailed picture of the possible campaign, the possible great accomplishment in promotion and selling, the possible large gain for himself. But the possibilities of the plan, born that moment and developed in his mind like the famed rose tree of the Indian fakir, seize upon him because of its bigness and plausibility rather than as a revenue maker. His bent of mind is creative. He sees acres of factories grow from the seed of the crude idea of the inventor, monster stores spring from the modest shops, great railroad systems develop from the line that as yet may be no more than a right of way. He is the great persuader of the twentieth century.

There are other kinds of advertising agents. There is the plodder, who might as well have been a clerk, a tailor, a farmer, or a machinist. He is useful, to a few men who are too busy or too lazy to do their own advertising. He is an inoffensive person, and does not often stand in the way of progress. His number is growing less and less. The periodicals do not like to do business with him, realizing the abortive quality of his initiative. The progressive busi-

The Agents

ness man, though small, cannot afford to submit to such a negative influence. There is the pettifogging advertising agent, who ekes out a precarious subsistence handling one or two accounts, brokering them through larger agents, and gratefully taking the Lazarine crumbs that fall from the tables of the more provident. He is disappearing, though, like the poor in the general relations of life, we are likely always to have him with us.

Out of the old conditions surrounding the business there has emerged a class of agents that are unique, not of the progressive nor of the reactionaries. They form a class which while they handle much business is on the whole sinister in influence, not in tune with the spirit of the day, a drag on the wheels of progress. They are the men who have sedulously cultivated the talent of taking tribute from both sides. They are the terror of the publishers and the despair of their associates. They chaffer and dicker and shave and pare and squeeze, and thus gather their substance. Some of them grow rich, some are respected, but few are liked. They do not keep accounts. Usually they must renew their list of clients every year or two. They encourage advertising that they may draw their commissions. They do not know advertising; they only know how to handle advertisements-- and collect their commissions.

The general practices of the advertising agents are constantly changing. There is nothing like a code for their guidance. They have just begun to cultivate solidarity—to feel the allurements of coöperative methods and work. They are just beginning to realize that idealism and altruism are the greatest money-makers in the advertising business, and that service is the magic word that brings success. Many of the leading agents have become very expert, in a formulation of their experience into a very good semblance of a science of advertising and in ability to read the public mind. They have become expert analysts of business conditions in general and of the particular problem in hand. To a limited extent they are efficiency engineers. They can assay a manufacturing business, with reference to the probability of the product becoming popular or salable, with more skill and certainty than the so-called efficiency engineers, because they always have in mind the capacity and disposition of the public to welcome and absorb the product. They have evolved a new profession, without an adequate name, and without a place in the economy of business that can be described or designated; but a profession that is concerned with formulating progress and fostering prosperity.

The advertising agents are in a difficult position, with respect to their remuneration. They work for the advertiser, and therefore, it is urged, the advertiser should pay them; but most of them draw their pay from the publishers. The publishers can well afford to pay them, but it is feared that if they do the agents will not work for the advertisers' best good. It costs the periodicals about as much, often much more, to get their advertising as they pay the agents in commissions; and they often have to solicit

the agents as energetically as they do the advertisers
who do not employ agents, thus paying two soliciting
expenses. If the publisher was content to await the
decision of the agent, he would be subject only to
the agent's commission as an expense on the business
the agent sends to him. But he is not content to rely
upon the good offices of the agent. He instructs his
solicitors to call upon the agent and urge the claims
of his medium; which, as a general proposition, is
useless. The agent, if he understands his business,
selects his list of mediums in advance of the publisher's knowledge of the account, and rarely changes
it. He is compelled to listen to the pleas of the solicitors, and does his best to placate and soothe them,
if he must refuse them the business. They spend their
time and his without sufficient return, and thus increase the solicitation expense of the publication, and
produce the economic fault of the publisher having
to pay two soliciting expenses for every contract he
gets from the agent, and one item of useless expense
for every contract that the agent has that he does not
give to the publisher.

This condition induces many publishers to believe
that the commission they pay to the agents should
be paid by the advertiser. There is some reason and
plausibility in the position. There would be more
justice in it if it were not for the fact that publishers fix their rates with the anticipation of paying
the commissions to the agents, and so provide for
their payment by the advertisers, in a roundabout
way, but none the less inevitably. As a matter of

Advertising

fact, publishers who habitually deal with agents provide in their schedule of rates for much more commission than they are ever called upon to pay, and thus actually collect from advertisers who do not use agents sums intended to provide for agents commissions.

There is no doubt that the present condition of the agency business is far from satisfactory, except in a few instances where the agents are large enough to impose upon their clients the theory that they render to them expert professional service, that must be paid for as is other expert professional service.

The business of the expert and successful advertising agent is different from any other expert service in business. It brings to the advertisers very big volumes of trade, and makes fortunes for such as know how to utilize it, and have the goods. The best of the agents give a service that is very much broader than advertising, covering all of the activities of the business, and many times it is the advice of the agent that transforms a doubtful and difficult business proposition into a great success. Yet the agent does not get any of the usufruct resulting from his work, except such as may be comprised in his modest fee or commission.

Some years ago one of the brightest of the advertising agents, who has always done a strictly personal business and immersed himself in his clients' problems, outlined his policy in the form of a "credo" which has never yet been improved upon. It is as applicable and apropos today as it was when it was

The Agents

written, and as it will be a quarter of a century hence. Here it is (on page 212), with apologies to the author, and regret that it is not in good taste to use his name in connection with it.

The matter of rates is alluded to in this credo, and it will be difficult for a non-advertising man to understand why it is of very great importance. It is getting to be accepted as one of the fundamentals of advertising that an advertisement is known by the company it keeps. It is also true that advertising mediums are rated by their practices.

The agents in all of the major cities have recently formed themselves into an association for mutual information and for the standardizing of their practice, as far as possible. This is one of the more important developments of the practice of advertising, since it is the agents that influence more effectually than any other section of advertising men. They are in constant personal contact with the advertiser, and have a large influence with publishers. An agent with a contract in his hand can do much to persuade a publisher to see the light as he sees it.

Some of the agents have for so long been running amuck in the advertising field that the agency business has suffered in repute. These men are being gradually eliminated from the business, or their practices are being reformed. There are two organizations among the publishers without whose recognition agents find it difficult to do business, and such recognition can only be obtained by those who are real agents, not merely representing one or two

AN ADVERTISING AGENCY CREDO

WE BELIEVE In strictly personal, professional service, of proved efficiency, as the only proper basis for an advertising agency or for agency recognition;

In an ethics of practice, in advertising as in other professions;

That agency service, broadly speaking, should consist in general business counsel, the preparation of advertising plans and copy, the selection of mediums, placing of orders, forwarding of copy, and auditing of bills;

In the abolishment by publications of all commissions to agents, and a corresponding reduction of rates to advertisers;

That the advertiser should pay all advertising bills direct, and a fixed sum for the agent for service;

In flat rates, prorated to one inch space, and the abolishment of reservation privileges beyond a date when new rates go into effect on new business;

In the adoption of standards, uniform rate cards for publications of the same class, and, as far as practicable, of standard forms for agency estimates, orders, and similar routine work.

The Agents

concerns, who are financially responsible and who will agree to conform to a few salutary rules. Agents do operate outside these organizations, by the favor of some publishers and by the device of brokering their business through a regularly recognized agent. This latter practice is becoming more difficult, as agents are not allowed to split commissions with their clients, or deal with agents who do split commissions. Periodical publishers, in their individual capacities, are also laying restraining hands upon the agents, and insisting upon perfectly open and upright practices. One of the big periodical publishing concerns lays the agents who may receive commissions from its treasury under very strict obligations with respect to their practices and their volume of business. As the pages in publications issued by this house cost advertisers in the vicinity of $5,000 each, per insertion, it means something like extinction for an agent to lose the commission privilege at its treasury.

There has in the past been a feeling that the agent was an excrescence on advertising, a leech, an unnecessary accessory. There was, a few years ago, much talk about eliminating him. Nothing came of it, except that the agents began to improve their practices and to be of real service to the advertisers and periodicals. Now there is no question of their utility, and that they have a place in the economy of advertising. The business would be thrown into great confusion if the agents were to be eliminated. They are not like commercial middlemen. They are creators, as well as handlers. They are contributing as much as any other division of the business to our knowledge of advertising. We know so little, and ought to know so much, that we are inclined to cherish every source of information, the agents as well as the associations of advertising men and publishers.

XVI

The Advertisement

The advertisement itself—the physical advertisement—is a more important element in the success of advertising than has as yet been fully comprehended.

The success of advertising depends very largely upon the impression made at first sight upon the readers of periodicals, and those who are brought into visual relations with all the forms of advertising. The first glimpse of the advertisement is the determining factor in its success. It will not get attention unless its primary quality is of such nature as to attract the attention of readers as they casually turn the pages of the newspaper or magazine.

It is not quite correct to state the matter even as negatively as this: So far as the advertising in a newspaper or magazine is concerned, the attention value of the reader is primarily less than casual. It does not exist. Not only does it not exist but there is a definite quality of other attraction that acts as a bar to attention to the advertisements.

The readers of newspapers and magazines are, usually, interested in the text, to the exclusion of the advertisements. The advertisements do not have an equal chance with the text matter. The readers' minds are intent upon the news or the literary contents, and are not open to the attraction of the advertisements in an equal sense.

The advertisement must, therefore, not only invite but compel the attention of the readers, if it is to be read and heeded. If the advertisement were certain of sharing the readers' attention equally with the literary text, more than half of the advertisers' battle would be won in advance.

People do read the newspapers and the weeklies and magazines. They buy them to read. How many of them read the advertisements is a moot question. If that proportion were approximately known to advertisers their problem would be vastly simplified. It is probable that the proportion of people who read the advertisements in the periodicals they buy, is higher than most advertising men will estimate, but vastly less than 100 per cent. If it was known to be 50 per cent there would be a very substantial basis for publicity work; though even then the proportion of readers who would probably be interested in any given advertising proposition would be small.

To get the attention of those people among the readers of advertising who may inferentially be interested in his proposition, and to make that proposition—his advertisement—so vital as to attract buying impulses in a proportion of the small proportion who are enough interested to glance at his advertisement—this is the task of the advertiser.

For the advertiser, the problem is to winnow the few and scattered grains of trade wheat from the great mass of chaff; to separate the one person from the hundred, the thousand, or perhaps the ten-thousand.

The first and most important thing the advertiser has to do is to get the attention of the one person

The Advertisement

who will buy his product. That one person is not looking for the advertiser's announcement. He is conscious of no need for the goods. He does not know that he is going to be invited to seek for the need. His attention must be arrested, and the need made plain to him. But first of all his attention must be secured. How?

If attention is to be sought by means of an advertisement in a newspaper or a magazine the problem is of a certain nature. If the billboard, the car-card, the electric sign, or any "outdoor" medium, is to be used, the problem is different. It is also different if any one of the many forms of "direct" advertising is employed. In the case of these latter methods, the primary attention of the person is assumed, and the advertisement may be shaped to offer its suggestion. In the case of periodicals the primary attention is the one thing that must be carefully studied. A person in a street car sees the car-card, or he does not. Nothing about the card can compel attention if the person does not voluntarily glance in its direction. It cannot be made to ring a bell to get his attention. But once the glance is sent roving along the rows of cards there is no news, no story, to compete for attention. The advertisements have it all their own way, and it is for them to put their suggestions at work.

The advertisement in a periodical is obliged to compete with the reading matter, and on uneven terms. The readers buy the periodicals for the reading matter. The advertising intrudes. It is esteemed

Good Display Without Effort

as an intruder, in the minds of many readers, and instead of being sought is often avoided. The advertisement has got to have some quality that will attract the uninterested attention of the reader, and in the instant of time his eyes are within its range.

It is perfectly clear that it must be the physical features of the advertisement that are to be relied upon to get the attention of the person who may, by some miracle, become a buyer.

It is not impossible to make the advertisement attractive, in form and general appearance. It is comparatively easy to do so, but it cannot be done simply by wishing. Some substantial part of the wastage in advertising is due to the manifest fact that so much of it is not attractive enough to induce potential buyers to look at it, much less read it.

It is necessary first of all to admit that graphic art is useful to the advertiser, and to admit that for many generations the eyes of civilized people have been trained to accept certain forms and reject certain other forms. The canons of art have been so ground into the consciousness of people that they now form part and parcel of their beings. While the love of art, for art's sake, is one of the attributes of culture, the love of artistic forms is a part of the normal life of most people.

Life, in many of its manifestations, is based upon artistic forms, and so solidly based that we have come to forget that they are artistic forms. There are certain conventions of architecture, for example, that are adopted into every form of construction, however primitive or simple. There are certain artistic canons that are at the base of all that is done in the way of art, and much that is done in all industries. Periodicals of all kinds are, generally, made in accord with basic art principles, and most of the advertising follows certain art rules and motives as to its dimensions and general characteristics.

Whatever, in advertising or other graphic object, is intended to appeal to the man through his eyes must respect the habits, constitution, idiosyncrasies, whims, physical capacities, of the eyes; and those qualities and limitations of the eyes have been fixed through generations of usage and habit. The advertisement must, to be precisely explicit, be a picture, to appeal to the normal human eye and arrest attention without the conscious assent of the owner of the eye. If the attention of the casual readers of periodicals is to be drawn to the advertisement in the paper or magazine that may be in hand, the advertisement must be attractive, along the lines of the habits and capacities of the eyes that are roving over the page.

Thus far the proposition is axiomatic: Anything must be attractive to attract. But, in the case of the advertisement, just what is it that must be done to get it the first moment of hospitable attention from the readers?

It must be made in accord with a few primary art principles, that are applicable to whatever is either artistic or attractive. It must be made in accord with the art canons that deal with proportion, balance,

The Advertisement

Copyright U. S. A. 1911 by The B. V. D. Company

A Picnic Is No "Picnic" Without B.V.D.

IN the country or in the city, outdoors or at the office, working hard or "laying off," you can make every day and all day a "picnic." Just put on cool B. V. D. Underwear. It is the natural, national *Summer Comforter*.

By the way, remember that *not all* Athletic Underwear is B. V. D. On every B. V. D. Undergarment is sewed

This Red Woven Label

MADE FOR THE

B.V.D.

BEST RETAIL TRADE

(Trade Mark Reg. U. S. Pat. Off. and Foreign Countries.)

For your own welfare, fix the B. V. D. *Red Woven Label* firmly in your mind and make the salesman *show* it to you. That positively safeguards.

B. V. D. Coat Cut Undershirts and Knee Length Drawers, 50c., 75c., $1.00 and $1 50 the Garment.

B. V. D. Union Suits (Pat. U. S. A. 4-30-07) $1.00, $1.50, $2.00, $3 00 and $5.00 the Suit.

The
B. V. D. Company.
New York

Well Designed and Good Copy

symmetry, harmony, color, tone, perspective, etc. It must be thus made in order that it may "look right." If it does not conform to these primary principles it will not look right; and if it does not look right people will not look at it.

The making of an advertisement, after the copy has been prepared, is strictly a work of art. Painting an oil or water-color, making a pen- or wash-drawing, etching a copper plate, or drawing on a lithographic stone, are not more truly artistic work than the designing of an advertisement. It is because this has not been realized, acknowledged, and enforced, that the wastage in advertising has been so high. The observance of art principles in the making of the physical advertisement would not operate to make all advertising efficient, but it would operate to substantially reduce the sum of inefficiency.

The first consideration in making an advertisement is the copy, and the object of the advertisement. If it is for a machine, and the copy is strong and solid, like the machine, the motive of the physical advertisement must be in harmony with the business and copy motives, and strong effects sought. It would not do to use delicate-faced type and border, nor to provide for too much white space. But the medium and its pages must also be carefully considered. It should not be the effort of the designer to produce an attractive advertisement, *per se*, but to try and devise an appropriate and agreeable avenue for the thought and motor impulse of the reader to travel in their journey from the reader to the advertiser's desire.

The Advertisement

It is not infrequently that the handsomest advertisement is the most inefficient. It is the desire of the truly able designer to accentuate the desire of the advertiser in such fashion as may be the most agreeable to the reader. To accomplish this the motive must be expressed in the language of the reader, so far as possible.

The general character of the advertisement must be determined by its commercial motive and the character of the medium in which it is to be printed. It must be shaped up in strict accord with the rules and canons of art made and provided by the habits of the generations. There is, for example, an inflexible law for proportions, of advertisements and all other objects of graphic art. It would be difficult, perhaps impossible, to explain why the "Golden Oblong" is the only rectangular proportion that is under all conditions agreeable to the eye. It might be possible to discover this reason, as it is still hoped that the nature, origin and constitution of electricity may sometime be revealed. It would be an academic search, and not of much account or interest to the advertiser, who is chiefly interested in the fact that the golden oblong, or golden section, is the proportion that is most pleasing for rectangles; and for ovals, crosses, etc., as well. The ordinary book page is usually a close approximation to the golden section. If it departs appreciably it is not agreeable to the eye.

The dimensions of the golden section have been computed by various learned men, who do not per-

A Bradley Type Composition

The Advertisement

fectly agree with regard to it. But for the purposes
of the advertisement designer it may be stated to lie
between the ratios 3:5 and 4:6. The former makes
a form that is usually slightly too long, while the
latter makes a form a bit too broad. There is a
mathematical formula for this figure, but if it were
to be given it would mean exactly what is here stated,
that the proportionate dimensions are between those
given. Another way to state it is that the base of the
figure should be practically one-half the length of
the hypotenuse of either of the triangles into which
the figure may be divided. That is, the base should
be about one-half as long as the distance between
one upper angle and the opposite lower angle of the
rectangle. If, for example, a double-column newspaper advertisement were to be designed, the columns
being the standard 13 ems wide, the advertisement
would be about seven inches deep. By the 3:5 formula it would be 7⅜ inches deep, while by the 4:6
formula it would be 6¾ inches deep. Either of the
three lengths will make a good newspaper advertisement, though so much latitude could not be allowed
in the case of a page for a good book.

This law of the golden section is the most important of the art canons that apply in advertising,
and in other ways than for the determination of the
proportions of space. The axes of an oval should be
to each other as the base and perpendicular of the
rectangular golden section; and the standard and
arms of the cross must be proportioned according
to the same rule. The point of balance of the adver-

tisement, with reference to the "weight" of the typography and decorations, is determined by the same rule—it should be at the point where the arms of the cross intersect the standard. We may almost say that the optical center of the advertisement is determined by applying this golden-section rule, and if the optical point of balance does not coincide closely with the mathematical meeting point of the two sections of a cross drawn within the rectangle formed by the boundaries of the advertisement it will not look right, nor be right.

It is a very simple matter, once the designer gets the idea that this golden-section principle applies intimately to all advertising. Its proportions are easily learned, and once learned they apply themselves to whatever problem there is in hand with almost automatic ease. In a short time one's eye becomes so schooled that there is no need of measure, or figuring of proportions. These dimensions seem to be natural to the eye, so much so that many people dealing with advertising are able to so proportion their work without reference to it that it is near enough right to "pass muster" with such as are not sensitive to fine gradations of excellence. But it is just the last eighth of an inch in the proportions of an advertisement that makes it right, or near right; and it is the right that wins in the race for results.

I alluded to the "weight" of the advertisement, meaning the mass of the tone, or color, involved in balance. It is plain that an object shaped like an advertisement, let us say, and intended to be hung on its axes in such a manner as to revolve freely upon either of them, must be so balanced with reference to its weight that it may be turned freely, and so that it will come to a rest at any point. An advertisement to be right must be balanced, with reference to typography, illustration, border, and decoration, so that it will rest evenly upon its axes, even as the physical mass of weight must be balanced upon its actual axes. Note the advertisements in any popular medium, and it will at once occur to you that those having the greater proportion of color below or above the point of intersection of the axes, do not have a pleasing optical quality—do not look right. No advertisement with the color preponderance in its lower area looks right; no advertisement with its chief attractive feature below or above the point of intersection looks right, or is right.

If I appear to insist upon careful consideration of this matter of proportion—the form of the advertisement, and the influence of the golden section in the matters of symmetry and color—it is because it is fundamental. If it is not right at the beginning of the advertisement, the fault cannot be overcome or minimized by any of the processes of advertisement building that come after. If the form of the advertisement is not right, type harmony, good color, right border, or any of the other physical elements, will not redeem or conceal the basic defect. They will, on the contrary, tend to exaggerate it.

Having fixed upon the proper dimensions and form

of the advertisement, it is important that the other building processes should be guided by a proper sense of restraint. Not that extreme restraint that

Fine Trade-Paper Advertisement

The Advertisement

affects minimum effects because of a false or artificial sense of modesty, but a restraint that will prevent the formation of a false atmosphere about the advertisement. There are advertising motives that require very pronounced arrangements of type and almost extreme sense of color, but as a general proposition it is easier to err on the side of too much and too strong display. Many designers, or printers, seem to think that the attraction of the advertisement depends upon the size or strength of the type—the general loudness of the physical motives, all along the line. A screech is heard, but seldom heeded. It is the quiet tone, the well-modulated voice, that really attracts that sort of attention that prompts action; that gets the response. It is the well-balanced, sane, attractive advertisement that attracts readers. The newspaper page that is filled with advertisements set in black type, with little of the white paper showing, is the page that the reader hastens to turn over, and hide from his sight.

Harmony and symmetry go hand in hand; the one referring more particularly to the tone of the physical elements of the advertisement, and the other to similarity of type and border design and the contours of the type forms. Harmony is best promoted through the use of types of the same family, or so closely related as to pass for the same family. The most effective advertisements are those composed in one series of type, using if necessary, the italic and boldface in connection with the normal, and being careful not to let capitals and lower case clash in

Advertising

line formations. Usually, it is better to use all capitals for all of the display lines, or none at all. One line of capitals in a composition made up otherwise of lower-case letters is almost always an offense to harmony, and often to symmetry. Capital letters were made to be used to begin sentences and to distinguish nouns. In advertising it is quite proper, and necessary, to use capitals for important words, whether or not they happen to be proper nouns. A judicious use of capitals in this manner assists display materially, being often more effective than "bull" type. But it is better to get the effects with lower-case letters. A piece of typography composed in capitals throughout, with lines of equal length and normal spacing between the lines, like a book page, is very hard reading. The eyes balk at it, and that fact is enough to discredit it for advertising purposes, for it is always to be remembered that the test for advertising that is back of and superior to all other tests is its readability—its agreeableness to the eye.

A very common offense in advertising is the use in the same piece of typography of varieties of type that are not harmonious, such as the injection of gothic display lines in company with roman faces, or *vice versa*. The so-called gothic types are undesirable unless used with great care and discrimination. They are radically different from the ordinary roman faces, and they clash. If they must be used, the whole advertisement should be set in them, body matter and all. It is possible to make an advertise-

Frohe Lieder

zu der Hochzeits-Feierlichkeit
des Fräulein Erika Meinert
mit Herrn Fritz Loße
am 12. April
1010

In den oberen Räumen des
Künstlerhauses, Bosestraße 9

ment which consists of a few display lines and no body of gothic type if it is carefully chosen and skilfully set. The Germans do it, but it is not often that we see an American or English advertisement thus made that is even tolerable.

The best advertisements we see in the great mediums are those set in simple type forms, using one series of type, with the illustration, if any is used, drawn to harmonize in tone.

Tone in advertisements is color, and it should be handled to help the general plan—to help balance, harmony, and perspective. It is controlled by the size and blackness of the type and border. It contributes to the general attractiveness of the advertisement, and it may be effectively employed to make the advertisement distinctive among others in the same medium. It should be so used as to bring out the chief point—the vital phrase, the line or word of the most consequence in a selling sense. Perspective is not often a factor in advertisements composed with type, but when it is possible to use it, it is important. Where there is an illustration the artist, of course, employs perspective with effect.

The logic of it all is that the designer of an advertisement should see his advertisement as a completed picture before he begins to assemble its elements. It is not so easy to do this. It requires that the designer shall have a pretty full knowledge of the business to be advertised, the scope and extent of the campaign, the mediums to be used, and complete mastery of all the physical elements that he must enlist. It is not necessary that the designer shall be an artist, in the sense of being able to paint or draw, though some facility in both adds to his efficiency; but it is absolutely necessary that he shall have a very clear knowledge of art and real sympathy with its many forms of expression, in order that he may make his advertisements in such fashion that they will make the best and strongest possible appeal to the readers, and attract the attention of people who would not look at them if they were not essentially attractive.

Aside from the strictly business motive, there is another very good reason for making advertisements as attractive as possible—the tolerance and pleasure of the people who buy newspapers and magazines to read rather than to be cozened into buying advertised goods. Some of the readers of papers and magazines do not object to the advertisements—some actually enjoy them, and consider that they are some real part of that which they buy. But, from the point of view of the advertisers, the advertisements are thrust upon the readers, through the connivance of the publishers, and it is one of the obligations of the advertisers to make their appeals as gracious as possible. As unbidden guests the advertisements should be in correct garb, and irreproachable in demeanor. If the advertisers paid all of the expense of publication, and were quite independent of the readers, they would still be obligated to make their announcements worthy of the houses they are expected to enter.

Whether an advertisement is welcome in the home

or not depends upon the advertisement. It may be so made as to be not wholly unwelcome, even if the message it carries may not be vital or altogether welcome. The peculiar nature of the advertisement, and its mission, makes it obligatory on the advertiser to use every endeavor to make it so physically attractive as not to be distasteful to those who buy the papers and periodicals, for the purpose of reading them.

Optics is of great interest and value to the designer of advertisements, as well as to the readers thereof. It is one of the elements in advertising that has not been thought too much about, or studied too much. Yet it is quite evident that an advertisement which is not agreeable to the physical eye is not going to get read up to the maximum. It is necessary that the designers of advertisements know what are the powers and limitations, the habits and preferences, of the normal eye; which is an organ with peculiar habits and unaccountable preferences. Its action and powers in reading concern the advertiser closely, since if he persists in making advertisements that are not agreeable to the eye, with reference to its natural powers or acquired habits, he is tempting fate to make his advertising inefficient.

The eye demands more than beauty—it demands ease, and forms that it can master. It is a peculiar organ. Its laws and limitations are just beginning to be understood. It has fixed habits for work. It has been adapting itself to type ever since type began to be made. In America and England, and in many of the other countries, it has become accustomed to

The Advertisement

the roman face of type, like those you are now reading. In Germany, and the Oriental countries, as well as Russia and some other countries, it has become accustomed to types radically different from the roman designs. It seems likely that the roman designs will eventually drive the other forms out of use. That is now happening in Germany, where the roman letters are coming into use and the old gothics, upon which the German types have been based, are being discarded. It seems therefore that the eye has selected the roman type forms. Advertisers may as well acquiesce, and use the roman faces.

It is the eye in its reading habits that most concerns the advertiser, however. The psychologists of the colleges are finding out what the eye can do in the way of reading, and their work is not only interesting but very valuable to advertisers. They have not been interested in this line of investigation long enough yet to have established complete reliable data for final and exact knowledge of the habits and limitations of the eye in reading, but there is available a body of results of investigations that is of great use to advertisers, and gives them about as much information as they need to guide them in adjusting the optical qualities of their announcements.

Professor Edmund Burke Huey has invented a delicate instrument which he attaches to the eye for the purpose of recording its action in reading. The chart on page 236 shows the action of an eye in reading six lines of 10-point, old-style type, the lines being 3 5/6 inches in length (23 pica ems). Professor Huey says, in explaining the diagram:

"The curve shows the action of the eye in reading six lines, preceded and followed by two free move-

ments of the eye each way, in which it was swept from one end of the line to the other, the beginning and end alone being fixated. The broad vertical lines and the round blurs in the reading indicate pauses in the eye's movement, the successive sparks knocking the soot away from a considerable space. The small dots standing alone, or like beads upon the horizontal lines, show the passage of single sparks, separated from each other by 0.0068 sec. The breaks in the horizontal lines indicate that the writing point was not at all times in contact with the paper, though near enough for the spark to leap across, as shown by the solitary dots. The tracing shows clearly the fixation pauses in the course of the line, the general tendency to make the 'indentation' greater at the right than at the left, and the unbroken sweep of the return from right to left."

It should be explained that this instrument fits the ball of the eye, with a cup carefully smoothed and pierced to allow the eye to see the print. The apparatus moves with the movements of the eyeball, and every movement is recorded as in the chart, by means of a delicate writing point operating upon paper prepared with a coating of soot, moving across the paper at a uniform speed and making the round dots at regular intervals.

It is seen that in reading the eye moves by jumps, not constantly. These jumps are called "fixations," and each fixation takes up, for the eye to read, a certain number of letters—a certain section of the line of type. This shows why short words are so much more agreeable to the eye. The chart shows that usually the eye hesitates at the end of the line, making there a shorter jump, or fixation. This indicates that the line used for this experiment was about as long as the eye was willing to negotiate. It was, in fact, a trifle too long, else the eye would not have faltered at its end. Evidently a line not more than $3\frac{1}{2}$ inches long is about the best length for the eye to willingly and comfortably read. This is a very useful and important item of knowledge of the eye for advertisers. If the lines of print are still shorter —the length, let us say, of the usual newspaper line— the eye would read with still greater ease and rapidity, provided other optical elements were equally favorable. If it were possible to use lines not more than one inch in length, and get good spacing between the words, it is very probable that many eyes would be able to read steadily down the column, taking each line at one fixation. This is practically impossible, owing to the difficulty of properly spacing words in such short lines. It is probable, therefore, assuming that the eye must travel back and forth from one line to the next, that a line from 3 to 3½ inches in length is the most agreeable for the normal eye, and consequently the most useful for the advertiser. As the eye must make a return trip from right to left, without reading, to pick up the next line, it seems sensible to assume that its journey from left to right should be about as long as its easy range for reading. Otherwise there would be too much jumping back and forth in reading a paragraph.

Another series of experiments by this professor, of peculiar interest to advertisers, was to ascertain how much reading matter the eye is capable of seeing at one fixation. That is, the eye in roving over a page of a newspaper or periodical is capable of getting an image of so much type, and transferring it to the brain in a form that gives the reader a definite suggestion. It was shown that the eye takes

The Advertisement

up in the neighborhood of one inch—an average of
.855 inch, to be exact. The experiment consisted of
having several people look at type matter through
an aperture opened and closed at intervals of one-
fourth of a second. This is valuable when the
advertisement designer is composing his suggestion,
or catch line. It should be only long enough to require one fixation of the eye in reading it. In other
words, it should be so short and compact that the
eye will take it in as it roves across the page, without

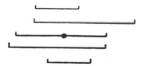

Diagram to show amount of printed matter the eye takes up at once.
From "The Psychology and Pedagogy of Reading," by Edmund
Burke Huey, A.M., Ph.D. Courtesy the Macmillan Company.

conscious effort, as it takes in small and simple
pictures.

Another experiment determined the speed at which
people read. Twenty people each read eleven pages
of a novel at a normal average speed of five words a
second. The advertiser may therefore compute the
length of time it will take to read his advertisement.
A page in a book containing 300 words will take one
minute to read. A magazine advertisement having
300 words can be read in a minute. One of the
fine-type advertisements of motor cars, that are now
favored by many makers, will probably take about
five minutes time to read. Are there not many readers

who will not spend five minutes reading a fine-type advertisement who would be willing to spend two minutes reading an advertisement like that on page 221.

It will be seen that this work of the psychologists to ascertain the habits and capacity of the eye is of much interest to the designers of advertisements, and enables them to make their work more effective in several essential particulars. These findings should be used in connection with what is known about the preferences of the eye for certain forms of type— for certain designs of type faces. There is no doubt, for example, that a catch line set in Caslon type, or in Century Expanded, will be more willingly read, and read by more people, than if it were set in gothic type, or some of the very black faces. And it will be easier read if set in lower-case type than if set in capitals. The catch line should be set in letters that are fairly full, not condensed and not too closely set together, if it consists of a single word, or two or three very short words. If it goes to the length of several words, or half a line, the type should be moderately condensed, about as is Cheltenham, and the letters should stand close together so that the words will each be a unit to the eye.

The question of the paper the advertisement is to be printed on must be one of the elements considered along with the optical question. Type looks well on certain papers, and badly on certain papers. As a general rule, old-style type should be used on rough-finished paper and modern on smooth papers. Caslon

The Advertisement

does not belong on super, English, or coated papers. It does belong on antique finishes, and on wove and laid. For supers, English, and coated papers modern-faced type should be used, except the new styles of old-style type that have been designed to use on finished paper, such as the Century old-style, and some of the new faces that have recently been evolved from the old Jenson type; which are properly to be considered as job types. The large sizes of job types, with old-style contours, may, of course, be used on finished papers. They have body enough to give the typography the necessary strength.

Appendix
"Truth in Advertising"

At the 1913 convention of the Advertising Clubs of America, held at Baltimore, the sentiment among advertising men leading to a radical reform in advertising practice was crystallized in a code. It formed the most vital of all the texts for the addresses and papers. Whatever may have been the announced topic, any speaker was certain of an enthusiastic reception if he made a fervid and uncompromising talk about "truth in advertising." A committee was appointed, and drew up a code, which was agreed to by sub-committees representing all of the different departments into which the delegates were divided, and finally passed by the convention in mass meeting. It may well be regarded, therefore, as the expression of some 10,000 men more or less actively engaged in advertising, and possibly as the expressed sentiment of the progressive business men of the country; and, as delegates from England, Canada, France, Germany, and several other countries were in attendance and participated in all of the formal actions of the convention, as at least the dawning advertising consciousness of the world. It is nothing against the movement for truth in advertising that some of the recommendations of the committee were not put into actual practice. It is quite possible that at that time the formal printed code of advertising morals was as far as the ordinary business man was inclined to go in the matter of consideration for the person who is the recipient of the benevolent attentions of the advertiser. The several codes follow, as they were reported in *Associated Advertising*, the official organ of the Association:

The Baltimore Code

1. We believe in truth, the corner stone of all honorable and successful business, and we pledge ourselves each to one and one to all to make this the foundation of our dealings, to the end that our mutual relations may become still more harmonious and efficient.

2. We believe in truth, not only in the printed word, but in every phase of business connected with the creation, publication and dissemination of advertising.

3. We believe there should be no double standard of morality involving buyer and seller of advertising or advertising material. Governmental agencies insist on "full weight" packages, and "full weight" circulation figures. They also should insist on "full weight" delivery in every commercial transaction involved in advertising. We believe that agents and advertisers should not issue copy containing manifestly exaggerated statements, slurs or offensive matter of any kind, and that no such statements should be given publicity.

4. We believe that the present chaotic multiplicity of methods of arriving at verification of circulation statements are not only confusing but inadequate, and that the time for radical revision of these methods and for standardization of statements is the present, and the opportunity for constructive work along these lines is given by the assemblage at this convention for the first time, of representatives of all the different interests concerned in this vital matter.

5. We believe in coöperation with other agencies now at work on this problem, especially in the plan of the central bureau of verification which has already been initiated by some of the organizations represented in this commission, and request the executive committee to proceed therewith.

6. We endorse the work of the national vigilance committee, and believe in the continued and persistent education of the press and public regarding fraudulent advertising, and recommend that the commission, with the coöperation

Advertising

of the national vigilance committee, should pass upon problems raised and conduct campaigns of education on these lines. We believe it to be the duty of every advertising interest to submit problems regarding questionable advertising to this commission and to the national vigilance committee.

7. We believe that the elimination of sharp practice on the part of both buyer and seller of advertising and advertising material will result from the closer relationship that is being established, and that in place of minor antagonisms will come personal coöperation to the increased benefit of all concerned, and the uplifting of the great and growing business of advertising.

8. We believe in upholding the hands worthy to be upheld, and we believe that each and every member owes a duty to this Association of enforcing the code of morals based on truth in advertising, and truth and integrity in all the functions pertaining thereto.

The Toronto Prologue

At the 1914 convention of the Associated Advertising Clubs of America, when the name and scope was changed, and the name made "The Associated Advertising Clubs of the World," the movement for better advertising conditions was formulated, and each of the departments of the delegates adopted some sort of a code. The convention itself adopted the following resolutions, expressive of the combined sentiment of the delegates:

Realizing that advertising has come to mean *service to mankind,* and that reciprocity is the greatest force in promoting the cause of human brotherhood and the world's progress, and

Believing that the new humanism in business demands recognition of the fact that all men are interdependent and have international responsibilities which can be best conserved by setting up ideals of conduct, and

"Truth in Advertising"

Wishing to secure to society a code of advertising ethics by means of which the members of each department of advertising can gauge their own conduct and also that of their fellows;

Now therefore, we, the members of the Associated Advertising Clubs of the World, in tenth annual convention assembled, at Toronto, June 25, 1914, do acclaim and publish the following *Standards of Practice* for the various departments represented at this meeting, and do individually pledge ourselves to coöperate one with another in living up to them as the best standards of right action now attainable for all those engaged in the business of advertising.

General Advertisers

Realizing our obligation and responsibility to the public, to the seller of advertising service, the advertising agent and our own organization, we, as general advertisers, pledge ourselves as follows:

1. To consider the interests of the public foremost, and particularly that portion thereof which we serve.

2. To claim no more, but if anything a little less, in our advertising than we can deliver.

3. To refrain from statements in our advertising which, through actual misrepresentation, through ambiguity or through incompleteness, are likely to be misleading to the public or unjust to competitors.

4. To use every possible means not only in our own individual advertising, but by association and coöperation, to increase the public's confidence in advertised statements.

5. To refrain from attacking competitors in our advertising.

6. To refrain from imposing upon the seller of advertising service unjust, unreasonable and unnecessarily irksome requirements.

7. To furnish to publishers, when requested, technical information which will help them keep reading pages and advertising columns free from misstatements.

8. To refrain from and discourage deceptive or coercive methods in securing free advertising, and to do everything

possible to aid the publisher to keep his columns free and independent.

9. To require standards for ourselves equal to those we set for others.

Retailers

Each head of a retail enterprise should dedicate his best efforts to the cause of business uplift and to this end should pledge himself—

1. To consider, first, the interests of his customers.

2. To insist on the courteous treatment of every visitor.

3. To permit no misrepresentation.

4. To discountenance careless, slurring or offensive statements on the part of salespeople.

5. To avoid misrepresentation or careless indifference in advertising.

6. To see that comparison values in printed announcements are with prices previously prevailing in his store, unless otherwise distinctly stated.

7. To avoid the use of such expressions as "Were $10," "Value $10," "Elsewhere $10," "Made to Sell at $10," "The $10 Kind," etc., where their use would give a misleading impression to the reader.

8. To resent strenuously—to the point of withdrawal, if necessary—the "make-up" of his advertising in a newspaper next or near announcements offensive to good taste or of a debasing nature.

9. To demand of each newspaper evidence of the approximate number of its readers (based on copies actually sold), their general location and character, and a statement as to how they were secured—by voluntary subscription, by solicitation, by premium or gifts.

10. To urge on newspapers that the same care should be shown in admitting advertising to their columns that would be shown in admitting news matter to their columns or in expressing editorial opinion there; that the newspaper should feel itself as responsible for the verity and propriety of advertising and news in its columns as for its editorials—always giving assurance that he will welcome just criticism of his own advertising.

"Truth in Advertising"

Magazines

We believe the magazine publisher is a trustee of the millions of homes whose entertainment and cultivation he strives to promote, and we therefore set up the following standards in the light and obligation of his trusteeship:

1. We commit ourselves, without reservation, to the Truth emblem of the A. A. C. of W.

2. We commit ourselves to ceaseless vigilance to see that every advertisement we publish shall measure up to that Truth emblem.

3. We commit ourselves to stand at all times for clean and wholesome editorial and text matter and free from advertising influence.

4. We commit ourselves to our advertisers and agents to maintain an absolute uniformity of advertising rates.

5. We commit ourselves to definite statements and to independent audits showing the quantity and distribution of our circulation.

6. We commit ourselves to maintaining the highest standards of character and capacity in appointing advertising agents.

7. We commit ourselves to continued opposition to free press bureaus and other agents for free publicity.

8. We commit ourselves to consider all matter for the publication of which we accept payment as advertising matter, and to so mark it that it will be known as such.

9. We commit ourselves to continue to give our constant attention to the physical presentation of advertising, in the way of paper, press work and general typographical excellence, to the end that advertising may secure its highest possible efficiency.

10. We commit ourselves to fair and friendly competition both toward our fellow periodical publishers and toward all other competitors selling legitimate advertising of whatever form.

11. We commit ourselves to work always with increasing zeal to do everything in our power to advance the cause of

Advertising

advertising as the great modern servant of the business world and of the general public.

Newspapers

It is the duty of the newspaper—

1. To protect the honest advertiser and the general newspaper reader as far as possible from deceptive or offensive advertising.

2. To sell advertising as a commodity on the basis of proven circulation and the service the paper will render the manufacturer or the merchant; and to provide the fullest information as to the character of such circulation and how procured.

3. To maintain uniform rates, according to classifications, and to present those rates as far as possible in a uniform card.

4. To accept no advertising which is antagonistic to the public welfare.

5. To effect the largest possible coöperation with other newspapers in the same field for the establishment and maintenance of these standards.

Business Papers

The publisher of a business paper should dedicate his best efforts to the cause of business and social service, and to this end should pledge himself—

1. To consider, first, the interest of the subscriber.

2. To subscribe to and work for truth and honesty in all departments.

3. To eliminate, in so far as possible, his personal opinions from his news columns, but to be a leader of thought in his editorial columns, and to make his criticisms constructive.

4. To refuse to publish "puffs," free reading notices or paid "write-ups"; to keep his reading columns independent of advertising considerations, and to measure all news by this standard: "Is it real news?"

5. To decline any advertisement which has a tendency to mislead or which does not conform to business integrity.

"Truth in Advertising"

6. To solicit subscriptions and advertising solely upon the merits of the publications.

7. To supply advertisers with full information regarding character and extent of circulation, including detailed circulation statements subject to proper and authentic verification.

8. To coöperate with all organizations and individuals engaged in creative advertising work.

9. To avoid unfair competition.

10. To determine what is the highest and largest function of the field which he serves, and then to strive in every legitimate way to promote that function.

Agricultural Publications

Believing that the growth of farm publications, both in a business way and in their usefulness to the farm reader, depends upon certain fundamental practices, the wisdom of which the agricultural publishers generally recognize, we set forth the following as an exposition of those practices:

1. To consider the interests of the subscriber first in both editorial and advertising columns.

2. To conduct our editorial columns with truth in a fearless, forceful manner, and in the interests of better farming conditions and better farm home conditions.

3. To keep them clean and independent of advertising considerations and to measure all reading matter by its worth to the subscriber.

4. To decline all advertising which is misleading, which does not conform to business integrity or is unsuited to the farm field.

5. To pledge ourselves to work with fellow publishers in the interests of all advertising and the ultimate success of the advertiser.

6. To accept cash only in payment for advertising and to maintain the same rates and discounts to all.

7. To allow agent's commission to recognized advertising agents only and under no circumstances extend the concession to the advertiser direct.

Advertising

8. To make editorial merit of our publications the basis of circulation effort.

9. To supply advertisers and advertising agents with full information regarding the character and extent of circulation, including detailed circulation statements subject to proper and authentic verification.

10. To avoid unfair competition and confine our statements regarding other publications to verified facts.

11. To determine what is the highest and largest function of the field which we serve, and then to strive in every legitimate way to promote that function.

Religious Publications

Standards of practice apply equally to all classes of publishers, whether they issue religious or secular journals; but they apply in a very peculiar sense to those who publish religious papers, and who should stand for the highest possible ethics; therefore—

1. We believe in truth in the printed word.

2. We believe that religion is the most vital force in the world and that the religious publications should conduct their affairs with a scrupulous desire to measure up to the standards which religion prescribes.

3. We believe that the religious paper should be faithful to its conviction and not allow business expediency to swerve it from its purpose.

4. We believe that religious publications should be kept up to date, editorially and typographically, and sold on their merits.

5. We believe in eliminating personal opinions in the news columns; in being a leader of thought in the editorial columns, that criticism should be constructive.

6. We believe that unreliable or questionable advertising has no place in religious publications.

7. We believe advertisers and advertising agents should be furnished with a verifiable statement of circulation.

8. We believe in discouraging the "Me too" form of advertising solicitation; every publication should stand on its own merits.

[250]

"Truth in Advertising"

9. We believe in lending a hand with all other organizations and individuals engaged in the movement of business integrity.

10. We believe in service—service to God, service to mankind—and that the religious publication is under obligation to encourage all movements for a better mutual understanding among men.

General Advertising Agents

Realizing the increased responsibilities of the general advertising agent, due to the enlarged scope and requirements of modern agency service, every agent should use his best efforts to raise the general standards of practice, and should pledge himself—

1. To first recognize the fact that advertising, to be efficient, must deserve the full confidence and respect of the public, and, therefore, to decline to give service to any advertiser whose publicity would bring discredit on the printed word.

2. To recognize that it is bad practice to unwarrantably disturb the relations between a client and an agent who is faithfully and efficiently serving such client.

3. To permit no lowering of maximum service through accepting any new client whose business is in direct competition with that of a present client without the full knowledge of both parties.

4. To avoid unfair competition, resolve to carry into practice the equitable basis of "one-price-for-all" and determine that the *minimum* charge for service be the full commission allowed to recognized agencies, and that no rebates, discounts or variations of any kind be made, except those regularly allowed for cash payments, and such special discounts as may be generally announced and available to all.

5. To conserve advertising expenditures by making investigation in advance of all conditions surrounding a contemplated campaign, by counseling delay where preliminary work must first be accomplished, and by using every effort to establish the right relation and coöperation between advertising and selling forces.

Advertising

6. To avoid, in the preparation of copy, exaggerated statements and to discountenance any willful misrepresentation of either merchandise or values.

7. To recommend to all advertising mediums the maintenance of equable and uniform rates to all advertisers alike and the maintenance of uniform rates, terms and discounts to all recognized agents alike.

8. To require exact information as to the volume of circulation of any medium used and specific detail as to the distribution of this circulation, both territorially and as to class of readers. In figuring the value of a medium to regard information as to the method of obtaining this circulation and the care in auditing this circulation as an essential consideration in estimating its worth.

9. To discountenance the issuance of agency house organs soliciting or containing paid advertising from owners of space.

10. To insure continued progress towards better professional standards, through the appointment of a standard of agency practice committee, to whom all suggestions shall be referred during the coming year, and who shall report their recommendations at the next annual convention.

11. To coöperate heartily with each division of advertising in its effort to establish better standards of practice.

Outdoor Advertisers

1. Every outdoor advertising plant must continue to refuse all misleading, indecent and illegitimate advertising.

2. Every outdoor advertising plant should refuse all advertising which savors of personal animosity, as ours is strictly an advertising medium.

3. All advertising contracts should be started on date contracted for.

4. Every client should be furnished promptly upon completion of his display with a list showing all locations, and plant owners should at all times assist clients to check displays.

5. Every outdoor advertising plant should be maintained in the best condition possible, both from the standpoint of appearance and stability.

6. All locations for outdoor display should be selected

where the traffic is such that it insures the best circulation for the article advertised.

7. Care should be exercised by every plant owner in the selection of locations so as not to cause friction either with the municipal authorities or the people of the neighborhood.

8. A rule of one-rate-to-all and one high-grade class of service to every advertiser must be rigidly maintained.

9. Every effort should be made to constantly raise outdoor advertising copy to the maximum efficiency in policy, ideas and execution.

10. Recognizing the great power of our medium, we should use it for the general good by devoting space to matters of general happiness and welfare.

11. We believe in close association among members of our own branch of advertising to the end that greater efficiency be attained through the interchange of ideas.

12. We believe in hearty coöperation between the outdoor advertising interests and all other legitimate branches of publicity.

13. We believe in the solicitation of business on the basis of respect for the value of all other good media.

14. We believe in dissuading the would-be advertiser from starting a campaign, when, in our judgment, his product, his facilities, his available funds, or some other factor, makes his success doubtful.

Direct Advertising

Every advertising manager or business executive in charge of merchandising establishments, also every advertising counselor in dealing with his clients, should dedicate his best efforts to making truthful, direct advertising an efficient aid to business and should pledge himself—

1. To study carefully his proposition and his field to find out what kind of advertising applies. The reason for every advertising failure is that the right kind of advertising and proper application for the particular product and market were not used. The only forms of advertising which are best for any purpose are those which produce the most profit.

Advertising

2. To bring direct advertising to the attention of concerns who have never realized its possibilities. Many concerns do not advertise because they do not know that advertising can be started at small expense. They confuse advertising with expensive campaigns and hesitate to compete with others already doing general publicity.

3. To determine the different ways in which direct advertising can be used to effectively supplement other forms of advertising and to so study the other forms used that the direct advertising may become a component part of the entire publicity plan.

4. To study the special advantages of direct advertising such as individuality, privacy of plan; facility for accompanying with the advertisement samples, postals, return envelopes, inquiry or other blanks; ability to reach special groups or places; personal control of advertising up to the minute of mailing, and other recognized advantages.

5. To strengthen the bond between manufacturer and dealer by encouraging the manufacturer to prepare direct advertising matter for the dealer, so well printed with his name, address and business card as to make him glad to distribute it, providing always the cost of special imprinting is in proportion to the benefits to be derived.

6. To take advantage of the opportunity to test out letters and literature on a portion of a list before sending them out to the entire list. Wherever it is possible for an advertiser to approximate in advance his returns from his advertising he has made his advertising more efficient. Direct advertising makes this possible. Testing out direct advertising campaigns in advance does much to remove the element of chance.

7. To consider inquiries as valuable only as they can be turned into sales. An inquiry is a means to an end—not an end in itself. The disposition to consider cost per inquiry instead of cost per sale has led many a firm to false analysis.

8. To give the mailing list its proper importance. Many advertisers use poorly prepared mailing lists, which are compiled in a careless, haphazard manner, and never take the trouble to check them up or expand them. Mailing lists should be constantly revised. Poor lists and old lists cost money in two ways: one by missing good prospects and

thereby losing sales and the other by money spent on useless names.

9. To encourage the use of direct advertising as an educational factor within their organizations with sales forces and dealers. Many concerns have raised their standards of efficiency through the use of letters, house organs, bulletins, mailing cards, folders, etc.

10. To champion direct advertising in the right way. General publicity and direct advertising are two servants of business and each has its place and its work to do. No form of advertising should ever attack another form of advertising as such.

Directories

The publisher of a directory should dedicate his best efforts to the cause of business uplift and social service, and to this end should pledge himself—

1. To consider, first, the interests of the user of the book.

2. To subscribe to and work for truth, honesty and accuracy in all departments.

3. To avoid confusing duplication of listings, endeavoring to classify every concern under the one heading that best describes it, and to treat additional listings as advertising, to be charged for at regular rates.

4. To increase public knowledge of what directories contain; to study public needs and make directories to supply them; to revise and standardize methods and classifications, so that what is wanted may be most easily found, and the directory be made to serve its fullest use as a business and social reference book and director of buyer to seller.

5. To decline any advertisement which has a tendency to mislead or which does not conform to business integrity.

6. To solicit subscriptions and advertising solely upon the merits of the publication.

7. To avoid misrepresentation by statement or inference regarding circulation, placing the test of reference publicity upon its accessibility to seekers, rather than on the number of copies sold.

8. To coöperate with approved organizations and individuals engaged in creative advertising work.

Advertising

9. To avoid unfair competition.

10. To determine what is the highest and largest function of directories in public service, and then to strive in every legitimate way to promote that function.

Printing

The members of the department of printing and engraving of the Associated Advertising Clubs of the World dedicate their best efforts to business uplift and social service and to this end pledge themselves—

1. To give full value for every dollar received.

2. To charge fair prices, viz.: known cost plus a reasonable profit.

3. To subscribe to and work for truth and honesty in business; to avoid substitution, broken promises, unbusinesslike methods.

4. To coöperate in establishing and maintaining approved business ethics.

5. To be original producers and creators, not copyists.

6. To be promotive, looking to the needs of the customer, analyzing his requirements and devising new and effective means for promoting and extending his business.

7. To place emphasis upon quality rather than price, service to the customer being the first consideration.

8. To merit the support of buyers of their product by living up to the spirit as well as the letter of these standards.

9. To develop by coöperation with other departments of the Associated Advertising Clubs an ever-strengthening bond of union to the end that the service rendered to advertising by the graphic arts may achieve its highest efficiency.

10. To aid in securing just and harmonious relations between employer and employed by establishing honorable conditions of employment.

Photo-Engravers

The photo-engraver, realizing the importance of his calling and the influence his products wield upon humanity at large and business in particular, volun-

"Truth in Advertising"

tarily sets up the following standards to serve as a guide in his relations with the public and pledges himself to observe them faithfully:

1. Being the interpreter of art and the manufacturer of a sales-producing medium, he commits himself unqualifiedly to truth.

2. To coöperate with all organizations and individuals engaged in uplifting advertising in all its branches.

3. To remove all mystery and misrepresentation surrounding his craft and his products, and to at all times welcome an opportunity to explain its intricacies to any one interested.

4. To study the requirements of his customer and to give the latter the benefit of his expert experience and advice, so that the buyer of engravings may consider them a sound investment instead of an expense, and profit by their use.

5. To serve the public to the best of his knowledge and ability for a fair remuneration.

6. To know his costs, and to maintain at all times a standard of charges that will honestly cover all costs of service rendered both in the preliminary preparation of work and in its execution, and to prohibit all gratuitous service or delivery of value without full compensation.

7. To stand upon the fact that the cost for making photo-engravings is the same for one buyer as for another, and that he who buys to sell again should charge his customers a fee for the value of the service which he individually renders.

8. To avoid the making of false promises and the disappointments and losses connected therewith, and to undertake to do no more than the plant is equipped to handle efficiently.

9. To educate the buyer of engravings in the technical knowledge necessary for him to buy them intelligently and to bring him up to an appreciation of "quality" in engravings.

10. To stand ready at all times to do his share towards improving, not only his own product, but to disseminate knowledge concerning its proper use, to raise the standard of advertising from the purely materialistic to the artistic

Advertising

and to add to its sales efficiency by all means within his power.

House Organs

In order that the house organ shall have a clear field for its development along lines of efficient and practical service in the advertising field, the following standards of practice for house organs is respectfully recommended:

1. To refuse to give or receive advertisements as favors or concessions, but only for a valuable consideration.

2. To charge, at a fair and profitable rate, for all circulation which does not tend toward directly carrying out the objects and purposes for which the house organ is issued.

3. To decline any advertisement which has a tendency to mislead or which is not otherwise in accord with good business practices.

4. To exchange circulation with other house organ publishers, with the idea and purpose of increasing the effectiveness of house organs generally.

5. To give full credit to those to whom credit is justly due for all subject matter taken from other publications.

6. To promote originality in the make-up and reading matter of the individual house organ.

7. To publish nothing but the truth.

8. To promote the spirit of optimism, thereby making the house organ always a message of good cheer and encouragement.

9. To avoid derogatory references to all competitors.

10. To have it understood and declared that the house organ publisher recognizes the rights and purposes of the respective trade publications, and that the house organ is not to supplant but to supplement the trade papers.

Titles in This Series

7.
Jean-Louis Chandon. A Comparative Study of Media Exposure Models. 1985

8.
Paul Terry Cherington. The Consumer Looks at Advertising. 1928

9.
C. Samuel Craig and Avijit Ghosh, editors. The Development of Media Models in Advertising: An Anthology of Classic Articles. 1985

10.
C. Samuel Craig and Brian Sternthal, editors. Repetition Effects Over the Years: An Anthology of Classic Articles. 1985

11.
John K. Crippen. Successful Direct-Mail Methods. 1936

12.
Ernest Dichter. The Strategy of Desire. 1960

13.
Ben Duffy. Advertising Media and Markets. 1939

14.
Warren Benson Dygert. Radio as an Advertising Medium. 1939

15.
Francis Reed Eldridge. Advertising and Selling Abroad. 1930

16.
J. George Frederick, editor. Masters of Advertising Copy: Principles and Practice of Copy Writing According to its Leading Practitioners. 1925

17.
George French. Advertising: The Social and Economic Problem. 1915

18.
Max A. Geller. Advertising at the Crossroads: Federal Regulation vs. Voluntary Controls. 1952

19.
Avijit Ghosh and C. Samuel Craig. The Relationship of Advertising Expenditures to Sales: An Anthology of Classic Articles. 1985

20.
Albert F. Haase. The Advertising Appropriation, How to Determine It and How to Administer It. 1931

21.
S. Roland Hall. The Advertising Handbook, 1921

22.
S. Roland Hall. Retail Advertising and Selling. 1924

23.
Harry Levi Hollingworth. Advertising and Selling: Principles of Appeal and Response. 1913

24.
Floyd Y. Keeler and Albert E. Haase. The Advertising Agency, Procedure and Practice. 1927

25.
H. J. Kenner. The Fight for Truth in Advertising. 1936

26.
Otto Kleppner. Advertising Procedure. 1925

27.
Harden Bryant Leachman. The Early Advertising Scene. 1949

28.
E. St. Elmo Lewis. Financial Advertising, for Commercial and Savings Banks, Trust, Title Insurance, and Safe Deposit Companies, Investment Houses. 1908

29.
R. Bigelow Lockwood. Industrial Advertising Copy. 1929

30.
D. B. Lucas and C. E. Benson. Psychology for Advertisers. 1930

31.
Darrell B. Lucas and Steuart H. Britt. Measuring Advertising Effectiveness. 1963

32.
Papers of the American Association of Advertising Agencies. 1927

33.
Printer's Ink. Fifty Years 1888–1938. 1938

34.
Jason Rogers. Building Newspaper Advertising. 1919

35.
George Presbury Rowell. Forty Years an Advertising Agent, 1865–1905. 1906

36.
Walter Dill Scott. The Theory of Advertising: A Simple Exposition of the Principles of Psychology in Their Relation to Successful Advertising. 1903

37.
Daniel Starch. Principles of Advertising. 1923

38.
Harry Tipper, George Burton Hotchkiss, Harry L. Hollingworth, and Frank Alvah Parsons. Advertising, Its Principles and Practices. 1915

39.
Roland S. Vaile. Economics of Advertising. 1927

40.
Helen Woodward. Through Many Windows. 1926